GOING, GOING, GONE?

ANIMALS AND PLANTS ON THE BRINK OF EXTINCTION AND HOW YOU CAN HELP

MALCOLM TAIT

THINK
BOOKS

A Think Book

First published in 2006 by

Think Publishing
Pall Mall Deposit
124-128 Barlby Road
London W10 6BL

Distributed in the UK and Ireland by Macmillan Distribution Ltd., Brunel Road,
Houndmills, Basingstoke RG21 6XS

Distributed in the United States and Canada by
Sterling Publishing Co., Inc.
387 Park Avenue South
New York, NY 10016-8810

Editor: Malcolm Tait
Deputy editor: Tania Adams
Sub editors: Colette Campbell, Rica Dearman, Matt Packer and Rob Turner
Design: Lou Millward and Mark Evans
Research: Jane Omara

ISBN-10: 1-84525-027-3
ISBN-13: 978-1-84525-027-0

Printed and bound by Printer Trento, Italy.
The publisher and author have made every effort to ensure the accuracy and
currency of the information in *Going, Going, Gone?*. We apologise for any
unintentional errors or omissions. The publisher and author disclaim any liability,
loss, injury or damage incurred as a consequence, directly or indirectly, of the use
and application of the contents of this book.

Cover image: Martin Harvey/Alamy

Going, Going, Gone? is dedicated to the wildlife of the world, and the many people who work hard to protect it.

With special thanks to Sonja Patel who first suggested the concept of this book.

CONTENTS

FOREWORD

Gerald Durrell once said: 'Animals are the great voteless and voiceless majority who can only survive with our help.' Now, many years later, I feel that animals are finding a voice and that people are listening to them. Endangered species have become articulate spokesmen for wider environmental issues. The polar bear on the ice floe said more about melting icecaps than the ice alone ever could.

Here at Durrell Wildlife Conservation Trust we are celebrating the 50th anniversary of Gerry's well-loved classic *My Family and Other Animals*. Five decades after this book began to inspire its readers to appreciate the natural world, is there anything for our 'family' to celebrate? The family embraces all living beings that share the planet, but things seem to be getting worse! New threats, such as genetic pollution and global climate change, are being identified, and the Red Lists of species under threat grow longer.

Nevertheless, I see a glimmer of hope. The world is awakening to some harsh environmental truths, and public backing for green policies is stronger than ever. Most heartening to me are the stories of the indefatigable work for threatened species, which we see so beautifully presented in this book. They reinforce the idea that something can be done by small, activist organisations or, even more effectively, by groups of like-minded institutions to stem the tide of species loss. The power of genuine partnership in conservation endeavours cannot be overemphasised.

The successes are not yet enough to turn the tide, but confidence is building and more good news is in the offing. A groundswell of public support for species conservation will inevitably follow, which in turn will put pressure on governments and regional bodies to meet the wider environmental challenges.

Let all our relations speak up at family meetings! May celebration and joyous song characterise family reunions, not funerals and dirges!

Lee Durrell
July 2006

INTRODUCTION

Sometimes it's hard to know the right thing to do. Almost daily, it seems, we're told through television, the internet and newspapers that yet another species is on the brink of extinction, that a habitat is disappearing, that the planet is losing its biodiversity. Life on Earth as we know it is going.

And, we hear, it's our fault.

We're using the Earth's resources too quickly; we're building on more and more land leaving less and less for the wildlife; we're polluting the seas and the lands; our actions are leading to unnaturally fast climate change: so many problems, so many mistakes, so much to put right... as I say, sometimes it's hard to know the right thing to do.

But, fortunately, there are people who are trying to find the answers. Millions of them, in fact. All around the world, there are charities and agencies working round the clock to change the tide. Between them, their staff, their members and their volunteers, they're working to protect delicate habitats and the wildlife that need them, and alter our perceptions of the natural world around us so that we live our lives more effectively, more sympathetically, yet no less enjoyably. Their task is a huge one, often a thankless one, and that's why we put this book together.

We wanted to sum up the world of conservation and all its complexities in a single, simple way, and show how everyone can easily play a part. We asked 99 conservation groups around the world each to pick one species, subspecies or habitat that needs saving, one symbol of the work that they do and the problems that they face, to write about it, and to demonstrate how you can help. And then, having received the 99 nominations, we rounded the book off with a nomination of our own, the Bengal tiger.

The response was tremendous. We heard from global groups such as the WWF and BirdLife International, and from tiny regional teams such as the Yellow-eyed Penguin Trust and The Seahorse Trust. We heard from conservationists from the US to the UK, from

Falklands to Gibraltar, from India to Jordan, from Australia to South Africa. The mix of wildlife was deeply impressive, too. Well-known animals such as the jaguar, lion, elephants and rhinos were nominated for the book, as were less well-known, but equally struggling species, such as the mulgara, golden conure, milky stork and Cuvier's beaked whale. Among the 99 you'll even find the kipunji, a primate so recently discovered that the photos you will see of it are virtually the first to reach print.

As you read through the list, you'll soon find your personal favourites among the species. You'll be moved by their plight, and by the efforts of the organisations that are trying to help them. If you're moved to do something to help one or two of them, too, then all the better.

The wildlife and habitats in this book are going: unless we do something, they will be gone. And the title of this book will no longer have a question mark beside it.

Malcolm Tait
July 2006

STATUS REPORT

In most cases, the species chosen are on the IUCN Red List, a global list of over 16,000 creatures that have been evaluated by The World Conservation Union, the world's largest conservation network. Where relevant, the status of the species is shown on its pages by one of the following criteria:

EXTINCT IN THE WILD: Known only to survive in cultivation, in captivity or as a naturalised population (or populations) well outside the past range.

CRITICALLY ENDANGERED: Considered to be facing an extremely high risk of extinction in the wild.

ENDANGERED: Considered to be facing a very high risk of extinction in the wild.

VULNERABLE: Considered to be facing a high risk of extinction in the wild.

NEAR THREATENED: Close to qualifying for, or is likely to qualify for, one of the above categories in the near future.

LEAST CONCERN: Widespread and abundant wildlife are included in this category, although they may be regionally threatened.

For more information, please visit www.iucn.org.

AFRICAN ELEPHANT

'IT IS ESTIMATED THAT MORE THAN 10,000 ELEPHANTS ARE KILLED EVERY YEAR TO SUPPLY THE ILLEGAL IVORY TRADE' IFAW

Elephants intrigue and fascinate us – we marvel at their size, their complex way of communicating, and their ability to 'never forget'. Yet time is running out for the world's largest land mammal. During the 1980s, Africa lost half of its 1.3 million elephants, largely to ivory poachers, before a global ban on ivory trade was introduced to stop the relentless slaughter.

Intense poaching, combined with the species' late sexual maturity and long gestation periods, has meant that many populations have been slow to recover, particularly in Central and West Africa where there are fewer resources available for their protection. As human populations grow, elephants increasingly struggle to compete for land, food and water.

IFAW works to protect elephants from commercial trade and increase their habitat. It funds research into 'megaparks' – creating a network of protected areas across Southern Africa, and provides vital assistance in the fight against poaching.

FACT BOX

COMMON NAME: African elephant

SCIENTIFIC NAME: *Loxodonta africana* (the African forest elephant – *Loxodonta africana cyclotis* – is widely regarded as a subspecies)

STATUS: Vulnerable

POPULATION: It is estimated that there are between 440,000 and 660,000 left in the wild (IUCN African Elephant Status Report, 2002).

LIFESPAN: In the wild, African elephants live for around 60 years.

RANGE: Sub-Saharan Africa, inhabiting areas of forest, savannah, grassland and desert.

THREATS: The ivory trade, bushmeat hunting, habitat loss and human-elephant conflict threaten to drive the species to the brink of extinction.

WHAT YOU CAN DO...

● Visit www.ifaw.org to find out what actions you can take to help save elephants from poaching and the ivory trade.

● Avoid buying anything that is made from elephants, such as ivory jewellery or trinkets, elephant-leather wallets, or elephant-hair bracelets.

IFAW.org

AFRICAN LION

'IN THE 1970s MORE THAN 100,000 LIONS ROAMED THROUGHOUT AFRICA. TODAY, THERE MAY BE BETWEEN 20,000 AND 30,000 SCATTERED UNEVENLY ACROSS THE CONTINENT' **BORN FREE FOUNDATION**

Lions are persecuted on all sides. Habitat has disappeared as human populations have surged; natural prey species have become increasingly scarce as a consequence of the bushmeat trade; disease outbreaks have killed hundreds of lions; local people have inflicted revenge attacks, angered by lion predation on livestock; poorly managed trophy hunting is removing at least 600 specimen animals every year.

Africa's lions are in crisis. The home of Elsa is in disarray. Lions have lost nearly 80% of their historic range. Although they are still found in 34 range countries, in 10, numbers are below 200 and these populations are regarded as endangered.

Born Free is tackling the illegal bushmeat trade; investigating the trade in lions either as hunting trophies, as live animals for zoos or for their body parts; working with local communities to encourage tolerance. An African task force for lions, backed by presidents and funded by the global conservation community, may be the only comprehensive answer.

FACT BOX

COMMON NAME: African lion

SCIENTIFIC NAME: *Panthera leo*

STATUS: Currently vulnerable (IUCN Red List)

POPULATION: Estimates range from 23,000-39,000.

LIFESPAN: Between 10-15 years

RANGE: Wild free-ranging populations of African lions now only exist in sub-Saharan Africa. Lions are found in a range of habitats including tropical/subtropical forest, shrubland and grassland, dry savanna and even hot desert

THREATS: Many, including livestock protection and revenge killing; human disturbances such as war and regional civil unrest; hunting for trophies and for bushmeat; outbreaks of disease.

WHAT YOU CAN DO...

● Joining the Born Free Foundation is the best way readers can support all its work and get more involved with the charity. To find out more about both Born Free and its lion project, please visit www.bornfree.org.uk, or email Born Free's CEO, Will Travers (will@bornfree.org.uk).

● To contribute specifically to Born Free's lion conservation project, you can sponsor the project directly at www.bornfree.org.uk.

AFRICAN WILD DOG

'FOR THE AFRICAN WILD DOGS TO SURVIVE, WE NEED TO PRESERVE THEIR REMAINING HABITAT' AFRICAN WILD DOG CONSERVATION

African wild dogs belong to a unique genus and are only distantly related to domestic dogs. These artfully painted dogs are highly social animals and depend on each other for survival. One pair in a pack will breed, and the group will often leave a baby-sitter to mind the pups while the rest of the dogs go hunting to bring back food.

Decades ago, the dogs suffered from a bad reputation and were shot as vermin throughout Africa. This dramatically reduced their numbers. Today, they are a valued and legally protected species.

Each pack travels vast distances, and some will journey over hundreds of kilometres to find mates. This takes them outside of protected areas and into regions where they come into conflict with people. For the African wild dogs to survive, we need to preserve their remaining habitat. By preserving these large areas we will also protect many other species.

FACT BOX

COMMON NAME: African wild dog, painted hunting dog, Cape hunting dog

SCIENTIFIC NAME: *Lycaon pictus.* Literally translated, this means 'painted wolf'

STATUS: Endangered

POPULATION: Between 3,000-5,000 left in the wild.

LIFESPAN: Seven to 10 years in the wild, longer in captivity.

RANGE: Sub-Saharan Africa – only six of the original 39 range countries in Africa now hold potentially viable populations.

THREATS: Loss of habitat, illegal snares set by poachers, shooting and poisoning in livestock areas, and it is thought they may pick up diseases carried by domestic dogs which can wipe out localised populations.

WHAT YOU CAN DO...

● Help raise awareness of the plight of the African wild dog. Find more information about the species and required conservation work by visiting African Wild Dog Conservation at www.awdczambia.org.

● Sponsor an African wild dog, or make a direct donation to a conservation project in the field. See www.awdczambia.org or email info@awdczambia.org.

AWDC

ALPINE IBEX

'IBEX ALMOST BECAME EXTINCT AT THE BEGINNING OF THE NINETEENTH CENTURY' ISTITUTO OIKOS

Once distributed all over the Alps, ibex were almost extinct by the early 1800s, thanks to centuries of active extermination. Intensive hunting for food, for its beautiful horns and because of the belief that parts of its body hold pharmaceutical qualities, had taken its toll.

In 1821, only one ibex population of 50-100 individuals remained in the Gran Paradiso area of the western Italian Alps. Thanks to the strict protection measures granted by the Savoia Royal Family, the colony started to increase. From this colony, the Alpine ibex has been successfully reintroduced in many areas of various Alpine countries.

Today, the species still faces problems because populations are isolated and have low genetic diversity: susceptibility to various diseases is causing drastic decreases. A common conservation strategy, based on a scientific approach at the Alpine level, is needed if we want to continue admiring the Alpine ibex as it bounds across the mountains.

FACT BOX

COMMON NAME: Alpine ibex

SCIENTIFIC NAME: *Capra ibex*

STATUS: Lower risk – IUCN Red List – Appendix III – Bern Convention – Annex V – EU Habitat Directive

POPULATION: A total of 39,300 ibex are present throughout the Alps (13,800 in Switzerland, 13,200 in Italy, 4,800 in Austria, 6,800 in France, 400 in Slovenia and 300 in Germany).

LIFESPAN: The Alpine ibex lives on average 10 years; individuals can reach more than 14 years of age.

RANGE: Mountain pastures at an altitude of 1,600-3,200m in the Alps (Italy, Switzerland, Austria, France, Slovenia and Germany).

THREATS: Loss of genetic diversity due to small and fragmented populations; diseases transmitted by domestic livestock; poaching for trophy (horns).

WHAT YOU CAN DO...

● Support Istituto Oikos programmes and research activities to conserve the Alpine ibex and other threatened species by visiting www.istituto-oikos.org, phoning +39 (0) 2 2159 7581 or sending an email to info@istituto-oikos.org.
● Find out more about Istituto Oikos projects for nature conservation and sustainable development. Join us at www.istituto-oikos.org.

ISTITUTO OIKOS

AMUR LEOPARD

'THERE ARE THOUGHT TO BE FEWER THAN 35 AMUR LEOPARDS LEFT IN THE WILD' ZOOLOGICAL SOCIETY OF LONDON

These beautiful cats, well adapted for snowy winters with their long, thick fur and pale colouring, are threatened by poachers and habitat loss. To combat these threats, the Zoological Society of London (ZSL) and its partners in the Amur Leopard and Tiger Alliance (ALTA) are implementing a conservation programme in Russia aimed at saving the Amur leopard from extinction. The alliance supports anti-poaching teams, a fire-fighting brigade, Amur leopard population counts and a large number of education projects. In 2005, ZSL and ALTA partners mounted a successful international campaign to stop a plan to build a large oil terminal in the Amur leopard's range.

ZSL and Moscow Zoo coordinate the European/Russian zoo breeding programme. Conservationists aim to reintroduce Amur leopards from the breeding programme into the wild in order to establish a second population within the Amur leopard's historical range.

FACT BOX

COMMON NAME: Amur leopard

SCIENTIFIC NAME: *Panthera pardus orientalis*

STATUS: Critically endangered

POPULATION: Only around 35 Amur leopards remain in the wild. Frequent leopard counts using camera traps and snow tracks indicate that the small population is stable.

LIFESPAN: Probably up to 15 years in the wild and a few years longer in zoos.

RANGE: A small patch of land in the Russian Far East near Vladivostok and the North Korean and Chinese borders.

THREATS: Poaching of leopards and their prey species, habitat loss due to frequent forest fires, economic development projects.

WHAT YOU CAN DO...

- Support Amur leopards! Donate directly to ZSL's conservation projects, and learn more about leopards at www.amur-leopard.org.
- The Amur leopard needs more friends. Tell your school class, your colleagues at work and your friends at home. This leopard is 10 times more endangered than its larger cousin the Amur (or Siberian) tiger.

ZSL LIVING CONSERVATION

ANCIENT WOODLAND

'ANCIENT WOODLAND IS ONE OF THE GREAT GLORIES OF THE UK'S NATURAL HERITAGE' THE WOODLAND TRUST

Imagine the outrage if a nationally important historic building was threatened by demolition. Yet nature's equivalent, our ancient woods, are threatened by destruction due to the pressures of modern life.

Ancient woods provide our richest wildlife habitat, and are home to more threatened species than any other UK habitat. These national biodiversity treasures are places of inordinate beauty, providing living archives with rich historical and cultural associations. Ancient woodland is finite, so what remains is precious and irreplaceable. Remaining ancient woodland is scarce and fragmented, covering around 2.5% of the UK, but the vast majority of ancient woodland has no national designation. Today these woods continue to be lost to road schemes, new housing, industry, quarrying airports, and threat from inappropriate forestry. The greatest long-term threat is climate change; many immobile species will not be able to keep up with the pace of change.

FACT BOX

COMMON NAME: Ancient woodland – UK native species like pendunculate or sessile oak; hornbeam, hazel, field maple, ash, wild service, hawthorn, blackthorn, spindle and wild cherry.

AREA: Only 341,100 hectares of ancient woodland survive in England; 60,600ha in Wales, and 148,200ha in Scotland. Remaining fragments cover only 2.5% of the UK.

LIFESPAN: Ancient woodland is land which has been wooded continuously for at least 400 years, often much longer. Some ancient woods go back to the last ice age, which ended about 11,000 years ago.

RANGE: Ancient woods and trees are thinly scattered across the UK landscape in urban and rural areas.

THREATS: Development of land for industry, housing, roads and airport expansion and commercial forestry.

WOODLAND
TRUST

ANDEAN CONDOR

'THIS ICONIC BIRD IS NOW ALMOST ABSENT FROM THE NORTHERN PARTS OF ITS RANGE' WILDLIFE CONSERVATION SOCIETY

A classic flagship species, the Andean condor is the iconic symbol of the Andes. The condor is also a very significant cultural reference and is revered by many of the Andean indigenous peoples. Sweeping majestically across high Andean landscapes on a 10ft wingspan, individuals have huge home ranges and political boundaries hold no meaning for the enormous condor.

Unfortunately the Andean condor is in trouble. It is almost absent from the northern portions of its range in Colombia, Ecuador and Venezuela. Habitat alteration and disturbance are important threats for the Andean condor, but they are particularly vulnerable because of their size, their conspicuous scavenging behaviour and the relative ease with which birds can be targeted. Although the bird is traditionally revered, some Andean communities blame condors for a portion of their livestock losses. Studies on population size and range are needed to help design appropriate conservation strategies.

FACT BOX

COMMON NAME: Andean condor

SCIENTIFIC NAME: *Vultur gryphus*

STATUS: Near threatened

POPULATION: Approximately 6,200 individuals.

LIFESPAN: Approximately 50 years

RANGE: Venezuela to Argentina along the Andes.

THREATS: Habitat alteration, direct persecution through hunting, nest disturbance and carcass poisoning from aggrieved livestock owners due to perceived and probable livestock predation.

WHAT YOU CAN DO...

• You can contribute to the conservation of the Andean condor by visiting and supporting the high Andean protected areas of Bolivia such as Apolobamba and Eduardo Avaroa. Log on to www.sernap.gov.bo. This will further enforce the concept that wilderness and wildlife can help pay for itself through ecotourism.

• You can also help save wildlife and wildlands by making a donation to the Wildlife Conservation Society, www.wcs.org.

WILDLIFE CONSERVATION SOCIETY

ASIAN ELEPHANT

'HUMAN SETTLEMENTS WERE ONCE ISLANDS IN A SEA OF ELEPHANT HABITAT. NOW THE SITUATION IS REVERSED, AND THE TIDE IS RISING' **FFI**

Venerated for its strength and longevity throughout human history, the Asian elephant is now in a precarious position, with little more than 5% of its original habitat left. Elephants need large, intact areas of forest to survive. Across its range, forest is increasingly fragmented by human populations, bringing it into more frequent conflict with people. Elephant bulls fall prey to ivory poachers; others are killed for meat or body parts for traditional medicines. Still others are domesticated as beasts of burden.

Flora and Fauna International (FFI) and its partners are working in Cambodia and Indonesia, where large areas of habitat remain. Working with governments and communities, FFI is protecting the forests for elephants and a host of other endangered species. As well as monitoring herds, patrolling and preventing trade in elephant parts, FFI is developing alternative livelihoods for communities that use domesticated elephants, and is responding to human-elephant conflicts.

FACT BOX

COMMON NAME: Asian elephant

SCIENTIFIC NAME: *Elephas maximus*

STATUS: Endangered

POPULATION: The population is estimated at between 35,000-50,000 in the wild (only 10-15% of the African elephant population).

LIFESPAN: Believed to be capable of living up to 70 years.

RANGE: Bangladesh, Bhutan, Cambodia, China, India, Indonesia, Laos PDR, Malaysia, Myanmar, Nepal, Sri Lanka, Thailand, Vietnam.

THREATS: Habitat loss and fragmentation; poaching for ivory and body parts; retribution killing for destruction of property and crops; capture for domestication.

WHAT YOU CAN DO...

● Support FFI's work to protect Asian elephants by calling +44 (0) 1223 571000, emailing info@fauna-flora.org, or by visiting www.fauna-flora.org

● Never buy ivory, even if it appears to be antique. Help reduce forest clearance by only purchasing Forest Stewardship Council-certified wood products, recycling and using recycled materials.

FAUNA & FLORA
International
Conserving wildlife since 1903

ATLANTIC COD

'IT WILL TAKE A FUNDAMENTAL CHANGE IN THE WAY WE MANAGE THE POPULATIONS OF COD TO BRING THEM BACK' THE OCEAN CONSERVANCY

They say cod is the fish that built New England. The original settlers arriving from Europe were amazed by the sheer quantity and size of the cod they saw in coastal waters. For centuries, cod was an economic staple in the north-eastern US and Canada.

Those days of abundance are long gone, however: the fish that built New England is approaching a state of collapse due to intense North Atlantic fishing pressure and mismanagement. In 1992, the bottom fell out of the Canadian cod market, and the fish is now commercially extinct there.

In the US, cod could face a similar fate if overfishing is not ended. Making things worse is a federal fishery council that often neglects science for short-term gain, hurting the future of the fishery and the fishing economy. There have been signs that the next generation of cod could jumpstart the population back to health, but it will take a fundamental change in the way we manage their populations to bring them back.

WHAT YOU CAN DO...

- Contact the New England Fishery Management Council (at www.nefmc.org) and tell them to follow the science and end overfishing.

- Find out more about The Ocean Conservancy's work on sustainable fisheries and ocean legislation at www.oceanconservancy.org.

FACT BOX

COMMON NAME: Atlantic Cod

SCIENTIFIC NAME: *Gadus morhua*

STATUS: Overfished

POPULATION: Recent assessments have shown a population decline of 20-25% since 2002, when populations were already severely weakened.

LIFESPAN: 20 years

RANGE: In the north-east Atlantic, commercial species can range from New York and New Jersey to Canada, although the species is now commercially extinct in Canadian waters.

THREATS: Overfishing, which can lead to other harmful ecosystem changes.

The Ocean Conservancy

Advocates for Wild, Healthy Oceans

AZRAQ KILLIFISH

'THE WARNING BELL FIRST RANG IN 1989 WHEN THE SPECIES WAS NOTICED TO BE IN DANGER OF SUFFERING FROM LOW WATER LEVELS'
ROYAL SOCIETY FOR THE CONSERVATION OF NATURE

The Azraq killifish is one of the most endangered species in Jordan. The warning bell first rang in 1989 when the species was noticed to be in danger of suffering from low water levels, and in the following years its unique habitats continued to dry up.

To make matters worse, five alien species were introduced to the fish's wetland habitat, eventually out-competing the species for food and breeding grounds, putting the little fish on the very brink of disappearance.

All is not quite lost, however: an ambitious project led by the Royal Society for the Conservation of Nature (RSCN) has literally brought the fish back from the edge of extinction. In 2000, the few remaining individuals were collected and looked after in artificial yet ideal conditions, while the natural habitats were restored. By 2006, the population had recovered from a few hundred to a few thousand. Yet so much more needs to be done to save this unique fish.

FACT BOX

COMMON NAME: Azraq killifish

SCIENTIFIC NAME: *Aphanius sirhani*

STATUS: Critically endangered (not IUCN classified)

POPULATION: The fish is endemic to a small wetland in eastern Jordan known as Azraq wetland. Population of the species is estimated not to exceed a few thousand.

LIFESPAN: The Azraq killifish lives for one to three years, and longer in captivity.

RANGE: It only exists in Azraq wetland.

THREATS: Water shortage and fluctuation, in addition to the high competition with alien species for both food and breeding grounds.

WHAT YOU CAN DO...

● You can help the Azraq killifish by donating to the Royal Society for the Conservation of Nature. Visit www.rscn.org.jo

● Find out about the extraordinary biodiversity of Jordan by visiting the Royal Society for the Conservation of Nature's website, www.rscn.org.jo

الجمعية الملكية
لحماية الطبيعة
RSCN

BARBARY MACAQUE

'POPULAR AS A TOURIST ATTRACTION IN EUROPE, BUT MISUNDERSTOOD AND THEREFORE VULNERABLE IN THE WILD' GONHS

You may be familiar with Europe's only wild monkeys, the famous 'Rock Apes' of Gibraltar. They are in fact Barbary macaques, which are monkeys, the only macaques found outside Asia. Asiatic macaques include the rhesus and long-tailed macaques that, like the Barbaries in Gibraltar, are tourist attractions in the temples of Bali.

In Gibraltar, the tradition of direct feeding of titbits by tourists has a negative impact on the health of the macaques and pre-conditions them to becoming urbanised and coming into conflict with the human population.

In the wild they are found as scattered groups of up to 70 in forests in the Rif, Middle and High Atlas mountains of Morocco and in open rocky habitats in both coastal Morocco and Algeria. They feed on a variety of plant material, including fruits, shoots, leaves and roots, as well as some invertebrates.

Changes in land use and other pressure from humans threatens in particular the wild Moroccan population.

FACT BOX

COMMON NAME: Barbary macaque

SCIENTIFIC NAME: *Macaca sylvanus*

STATUS: Vulnerable

POPULATION: There are about 240 living on the Rock of Gibraltar, probably introduced from Morocco at least 200 years ago. The total population in North Africa is no more than 10,000.

LIFESPAN: Up to 25 years, probably less in a truly wild state.

RANGE: Formerly found throughout most of North Africa, they now only occur in Morocco and Algeria, as well as Gibraltar.

THREATS: Habitat degradation and loss, especially in the Middle Atlas, where overgrazing by domestic animals and difficulty in accessing water points due to increasing human pressure is reducing the quality of the habitat. This is causing them to damage cedars through the eating of bark, making them unpopular among the human population. There is also the problem of the capture of macaque infants for sale as pets in southern Europe.

WHAT YOU CAN DO...

● Enquire about ecotourism trips to Morocco with an emphasis on natural habitats and seeing the macaques in the wild. This will increase their value to the local community.

● Find out more about the work of the Gibraltar Ornithological & Natural History Society in Gibraltar and Morocco by visiting www.gonhs.org or by calling +350 72639.

BECHSTEIN'S BAT

'BATS HAVE SUFFERED MAJOR DECLINES FROM HUMAN ACTIVITIES THAT HAVE CAUSED HABITATS TO BE DESTROYED AND THE INSECTS THEY FEED ON TO BECOME SCARCE' BAT CONSERVATION TRUST

There are around 1,100 species of bats worldwide, making up about one fifth of all mammals, yet relatively little is known about many of these incredible animals and at least 20% are threatened with extinction. Bats inspire strong passions, from great enthusiasm to fear and misunderstanding.

The Bechstein's bat is one of Europe and the UK's rarest and most secretive bat species. It depends heavily on mature deciduous woodland for its survival; roosting in woodpecker holes and crevices in trees, and feeding on woodland insects, which it hunts using the specialised sense of echolocation.

Its preference for living in woodlands means that the Bechstein's bat has suffered greatly from land use change that has caused extensive loss and fragmentation of woodland. Sensitive management of remaining mature woodland and measures to protect and connect woodlands are essential for the conservation of this species.

WHAT YOU CAN DO...

• Support the work of the Bat Conservation Trust in conserving this and other bat species by becoming a member. Find out more online by visiting www.bats.org.uk or by phoning the National Bat Helpline on +44 (0) 845 1300 228.

• Take part in the National Bat Monitoring Programme to help track the progress of the UK's bat populations. You don't need to be an expert. Visit www.bats.org.uk.

FACT BOX

COMMON NAME: Bechstein's bat

SCIENTIFIC NAME: *Myotis bechsteinii*

STATUS: Vulnerable (Global IUCN status 2006)

POPULATION: The exact worldwide population of the Bechstein's bat is not known. However, we do know that Bechstein's bat has gone from being one of the commonest UK species to one of the rarest, due largely to the destruction of ancient woodland that once covered much of the UK. It is now thought to number as few as 1,500 individuals.

LIFESPAN: Bechstein's bats have been recorded as living up to 21 years.

RANGE: Bechstein's bat is widespread, yet rare, across continental Europe.

THREATS: Destruction of ancient woodland, inappropriate woodland management resulting in loss of roost trees and reduced insect biodiversity, landscape fragmentation through removal of hedgerows thereby diminishing connectivity between woodland areas.

Bat Conservation Trust

BENGAL TIGER

'IN 70 YEARS, THREE SUBSPECIES OF TIGER HAVE BECOME EXTINCT. IT WOULD BE A TRAVESTY TO LET THE BENGAL TIGER GO THE SAME WAY' THINK PUBLISHING

The most iconic of the tiger subspecies, Bengal tigers, which are nominated here by the book's publishers, can be distinguished from other subspecies by their short reddish-orange fur crossed with narrow brown, grey or black stripes. This pattern is unique for each individual.

Found in Bengal's varied jungle, humid evergreen forests and mangrove swamps, this magnificent animal faces an uncertain future. With the population of India increasing beyond a billion people, the natural habitats of the tiger are being destroyed to meet the increasing demand for human settlements.

The other major threat faced by Bengals is poaching. The tiger has long been prized for its supposed healing properties and their bones are used in India and China as aphrodisiacs and medicines. They are also poached for their furs.

Over the last 20 years, the population has declined dramatically. Yet with renewed conservation work, this beautiful animal can still be saved.

FACT BOX

COMMON NAME: Bengal Tiger

SCIENTIFIC NAME: *Panthera tigris tigris*

STATUS: Endangered

POPULATION: Between 3,000 and 4,500

LIFESPAN: 15-20 years

RANGE: Primarily the mangrove swamps, humid forest and swamplands of the Sunderbans in India. Sparse populations exist in Bangladesh, Bhutan, Myanmar, Nepal and China.

THREATS: Habitat alteration, direct persecution through hunting.

WHAT YOU CAN DO...

• Support The Tiger Foundation's work with tigers by raising funds or volunteering. Visit www.tigerfdn.ca to find out more about what you can do to help. You can also become a member of The Tiger Foundation to find out about their latest initiatives.

• Avoid buying products derived from tigers.

BLACK-BROWED ALBATROSS

'NINETEEN OF THE 21 SPECIES OF ALBATROSS ARE NOW THREATENED WITH EXTINCTION' FALKLANDS CONSERVATION

Albatrosses are magnificent seabirds, they are renowned for roaming vast distances across the South Atlantic Ocean. They are also praised by poets and revered by sailors. Yet 19 of the 21 species are now threatened with extinction.

Most of the world's population of the beautiful black-browed albatross is found on the Falkland Islands where it has suffered a 9% decline with 38,500 breeding pairs disappearing in the past 10 years. The greatest threat to their survival is from commercial fishing. Many are killed in long-line fisheries when birds get caught on the baited hooks, are dragged underwater and drowned. Measures developed to reduce these seabird deaths have had a dramatic effect on albatross survival in Falkland Islands waters. But most are killed far from their breeding grounds and unless steps are taken at an international level, and fishermen are made more aware of the problem, the albatross will continue to decline.

WHAT YOU CAN DO...

- Find out more about the work of Falklands Conservation by visiting www.falklandsconservation.com.

- Support BirdLife International's Global Seabird Programme (http://seabirds.birdlife.org), working to influence the development and content of international agreements, which establish the legal obligations for countries to protect seabirds, both on land and in their fisheries.

FACT BOX

COMMON NAME: Black-browed albatross

SCIENTIFIC NAME: *Thalassarche melanophrys*

STATUS: Endangered

POPULATION: 618,153 pairs, with 399,416 in the Falklands Islands.

LIFESPAN: About 30 years.

RANGE: Circumpolar between 65°S and 20°S, breeding on subantarctic islands, including the Falkland Islands, South Georgia and islands found off southern South America.

THREATS: Commercial fisheries: it is one of the most frequently killed species in many long-line fisheries, and killed in significant numbers by trawl fisheries.

FALKLANDS CONSERVATION

BLACK RHINO

'ANCESTORS OF MODERN RHINOS WALKED WITH DINOSAURS. WILL THE TWENTY-FIRST CENTURY BE THE SPECIES' LAST STAND?' DAVID SHEPHERD WILDLIFE FOUNDATION

Rhinos have lived on earth for 40 million years but it has taken just half of one century to bring each of the five remaining species to the brink of extinction. And none have disappeared faster than Africa's black rhinos. Hunted and slaughtered in their thousands through the 1970s and 1980s, their numbers crashed until only a few thousand now survive in heavily protected reserves. Ironically, a group of rhino is called a 'crash'!

Possessing two horns, black rhinos are normally solitary animals, preferring dense thickets for browsing, using their prehensile top lip. With weak eyesight, they are naturally nervous and, if disturbed, will charge any perceived threat. With African rhino horn fetching higher prices than gold, it is a lucrative market for poachers. Tough anti-poaching measures and stamping out the illegal consumer market are the only ways to ensure that rhinos still survive in the wild at the end of the twenty-first century.

WHAT YOU CAN DO...

• Find out more/donate to the critical anti-poaching, community education and monitoring work of the David Shepherd Wildlife Foundation (DSWF) by visiting www.davidshepherd.org or by phoning +44 (0) 1483 272323.

• Adopt a rhino through DSWF. Namibia is home to one of the last surviving strongholds of truly wild black rhinos. 'Matilda' lives in the Namib desert and is quite a character!

FACT BOX

COMMON NAME: Black rhino

SCIENTIFIC NAME: *Diceros bicornis*

STATUS: Critically endangered

POPULATION: The wild population has declined by a catastrophic 97.5% from around 100,000 in the early 1960s to an estimated 3,600 today, making it the fastest-disappearing large mammal in the world.

LIFESPAN: Black rhinos can live up to 30-40 years in the wild.

RANGE: Sustainable populations of black rhinos survive in South Africa, Namibia, Kenya and Tanzania with a relic population in Zimbabwe and plans to reintroduce them to other previous range states.

THREATS: The main threat to rhinos is poaching for their horns, both as decorative dagger handles in Yemen, and as an ingredient in Traditional Chinese Medicines in the Far East. They are further threatened by habitat loss and human disturbance.

David Shepherd
Wildlife Foundation

BOWHEAD WHALE

'PRIOR TO THE ONSLAUGHT OF COMMERCIAL WHALING, THERE WERE PROBABLY OVER 50,000 BOWHEAD WHALES WORLDWIDE. TODAY THERE ARE ABOUT 8,000' ALASKA WILDERNESS LEAGUE

Bowhead whales are one of the most majestic animals that have ever lived on Earth. One of the largest of the great whale species, the bowhead whale is found in the high latitudes of the northern hemisphere, making this species especially conditioned to live in cold water and ice.

Prior to the onslaught of commercial whaling in the seventeenth century, it is believed there were over 50,000 bowhead whales worldwide. Unsustainable commercial whaling practices devastated populations until they were finally protected under an international ban on commercial whaling in 1987. Their total number is now estimated to be at about 8,000.

Increased offshore oil and gas development poses another major threat to this vulnerable species. In addition, bowhead whales are at risk of ingesting krill and zooplankton contaminated by harmful discharge from oil and gas activities. Consuming contaminated sea life is a major threat to large marine mammals such as whales since the chemicals will accumulate in their blubber over time.

WHAT YOU CAN DO...

• Find out how the Alaska Wilderness League is fighting to protect Alaska's wildlife and public lands and oceans at www.alaskawild.org, or by calling +1 (202) 544 5205.

• Urge your lawmakers to stop increased offshore oil and gas drilling in the Arctic and preserve the habitat of the bowhead whale, and urge the US Minerals Management Service not to include known bowhead whale habitat in the planning areas of its next oil and gas leasing plan for the Beaufort and Chukchi seas.

FACT BOX

COMMON NAME: Bowhead Whale

SCIENTIFIC NAME: *Balaena mysticetus*

STATUS: Endangered (not IUCN)

POPULATION: Presently, the number of bowhead whales of the Chukchi, Beaufort and Bering seas is thought to exceed 8,000 while those of the eastern Canadian Arctic and of the Okhotsk Sea in eastern Russia are thought to only be in the hundreds.

LIFESPAN: Bowhead whales were thought to have had an average lifespan of 50-60 years, but recent research indicates that some whales have lived to be over 200, making them the world's oldest mammals.

RANGE: Bowhead whales are found exclusively in arctic regions. Alaskan populations spend the majority of their time in the Bering Sea during winter then migrate to the Chukchi and Beaufort seas in spring.

THREATS: Whaling, increased ship traffic, noise pollution from seismic exploration, increased offshore platforms, chemical pollution and oil operational discharge, ship collisions and oil spills.

ALASKA WILDERNESS LEAGUE

BROWN HYENA

'THIS CRYPTIC ANIMAL USUALLY LIVES AROUND US WITHOUT BEING NOTICED, BUT ONCE DETECTED, IT IS GENERALLY MISUNDERSTOOD AND THEREFORE IN DANGER' BROWN HYENA RESEARCH PROJECT

Not many people have ever seen brown hyenas or even know of their existence. These large African carnivores are predominant scavengers, and are therefore of major importance to keep the environment clean. Their sense of smell is extremely well developed and they can detect carcasses over great distances. However, the brown hyena's capability of finding carrion quickly is one of their greatest problems. Outside of protected areas, they are often found first at carcasses and often blamed for killing livestock, resulting in their persecution.

Brown hyenas have large home ranges of up to 1,500km² and they travel 30-40km per day. While travelling, they often have to cross roads and are frequently hit and killed by vehicles.

A lack of knowledge about brown hyenas within local communities also exposes the creatures to risks because they are feared and killed, or they are injured in snares.

WHAT YOU CAN DO...

● Become a friend of the Brown Hyena Research Project. Send an email to strandwolf@iway.na, with BHRP Friend in the subject line. Friends receive our newsletter, and the donations and fees help to run the conservation projects in Namibia.

● Adopt or sponsor a brown hyena (email strandwolf@iway.na or visit www.strandwolf.org.za). Donations contribute to radio tracking your adopted or sponsored hyena.

FACT BOX

COMMON NAME: Brown hyena

SCIENTIFIC NAME: *Parahyaena brunnea*

STATUS: International: lower risk, near threatened. Namibia: insufficiently known (vulnerable or endangered)

POPULATION: The entire population is estimated at 5,000-8,000 animals. Namibia has a population size of around 800-1,200 animals.

LIFESPAN: Lifespan of brown hyenas in the wild is unknown, but some wild animals reach ages of 16 years. They can reach over 20 years in captivity.

RANGE: Brown hyenas occur in the southern African sub-region.

THREATS: Habitat destruction and fragmentation, human/carnivore conflict resulting in poisoning and trapping, road kills.

BROWN HYENA
research project
Skeleton Coast - Lüderitz

BUMBLEBEES

'ABOUT HALF OF BRITAIN'S SOCIAL BUMBLEBEE SPECIES ARE IN DIRE STRAITS' BUGLIFE

Few invertebrates have the appeal of bumblebees. It is not just their fluffy appearance that charms; their love of flowers and soft bumbling ways also endear them to us. While there are 270 species of bee in the UK, it is the bumblebees that are best known, but all is not well. In the last 50 years, 10 of the species have undergone massive declines and one, the short-haired bumblebee (*Bombus subterraneus*), became extinct in about 1990. About half of the social bumblebee species are therefore in dire straits.

The economic impacts to agriculture from the loss of natural pollinators is well known in America, and in Europe, where 38% of bees and hoverflies are in decline, the first evidence of suppressed agricultural productivity due to the lack of pollination is coming to light. The decline of bumblebees is marching hand in hand with the loss of wildflowers: we may not find out what is cause and what is effect until it is too late.

FACT BOX

COMMON NAME: Bumblebees

SCIENTIFIC NAME: *Bombus* species

STATUS: Declining – several are UK Biodiversity Action priorities

POPULATION: Ten species are disappearing – the Shrill-carder bee (*Bombus sylvarum*) and the great yellow bumblebee (*Bombus distinguendus*) being two notable examples.

LIFESPAN: Bumblebees are creatures with an annual lifecycle. The nest dies out at the end of the warmer months, and the young queen survives the winter to found her colony at the start of the following year. Bumblebees do not occur in parts of the world with no winter.

RANGE: Throughout the UK, but some species now very restricted.

THREATS: Loss of wildflowers, pesticides, development, climate change and an over-tidy countryside.

BUTTON CORAL

'THE DECLINE OF CORAL AROUND THE WORLD HAS LARGELY HAPPENED WITHIN A SINGLE HUMAN LIFETIME' CORAL CAY CONSERVATION

Coral reefs are extraordinary things. The nature of the relationship between the coral animals (polyps) and the microscopic algae that live within their body tissues allows them to recycle nutrients between them, enabling reefs to form in nutrient-poor waters that would normally be largely devoid of life. Reefs are composed of the skeletons of countless ancestral coral polyps built up over thousands (and sometimes millions) of years. These reefs support all of the other colourful life we associate with tropical seas, and around 500 million people gain a substantial portion of their livelihoods from them. However, when the corals die, the reef dies too: today, around 25% of our reefs are dead or dying, with a further 30% severely threatened.

Startlingly, this decline has largely happened within a single human lifetime. Although it would be unfair to choose a single species of the 800 or so reef-building corals as being more at risk, *Cynarina lacrymalis* is a beautiful ambassador.

WHAT YOU CAN DO...

• Don't touch them, walk on them or take bits home. Importing corals (including coral jewellery) without a permit is illegal. Find out more at www.coralcay.org

• Don't buy marine souvenirs, such as turtle, conch, or sea-urchin shells, even if you get reassurances from the vendor, these are almost invariably harvested directly from the reef and this contributes to reef degradation.

CORAL CAY CONSERVATION

Expeditions

CERULEAN WARBLER

'THE SIGHT OF THE CERULEAN WARBLER IS BECOMING EVER RARER AS ITS POPULATION CONTINUES A STEADY 40-YEAR DOWNWARD TREND'
AMERICAN BIRD CONSERVANCY

Look into the canopy of a mature forest in the eastern United States during spring, and you might see a beautiful bright blue bird flitting among the branches. But the sight of the cerulean warbler is becoming ever rarer as its population continues a 40-year downward trend.

Habitat loss is the main problem. Damaging land use practices on US breeding grounds are devastating hundreds of thousands of acres of forest and streamside habitat. Land conversion to coffee plantations on its wintering grounds is also affecting the species. But American Bird Conservancy (ABC) is working hard to ensure its survival. In conjunction with Fundación ProAves in Colombia, ABC created the first reserve for the species in Latin America, and is working with farmers to encourage coffee production that leaves habitat intact. ABC is also opposing mountain-top mining proposals in East US and working to ensure that lighting on tall towers does not pose a threat to this and other songbirds during their migration.

FACT BOX

COMMON NAME: Cerulean warbler

SCIENTIFIC NAME: *Dendroica cerulea*

STATUS: Vulnerable

POPULATION: Between 5-600,000, but declining at a rate of 4.5% per year

LIFESPAN: Five to eight years

RANGE: Breeds in the north-eastern and central parts of the United States, from the Atlantic Coast west to Iowa, as far north as Ontario and as far south as Arkansas. Winters on the slopes of the Andes and montane forests of northern South America.

THREATS: Habitat loss and degradation on both its breeding and wintering grounds are the main threats, but other hazards, such as collisions with communication towers may also be contributing to population declines.

WHAT YOU CAN DO...

● Join ABC, the only organisation working solely to conserve wild birds and their habitats throughout the Americas. You can visit the website (www.abcbirds.org) and purchase cerulean warbler conservation stamps. These can be used to mail letters to and from anywhere in the United States.

● Purchase only 'shade coffee' grown in plantations that leave habitat for cerulean warblers and other birds.

AMERICAN BIRD CONSERVANCY

CHEETAH

'THE WORLD'S FASTEST LAND ANIMAL IS RUNNING OUT OF TIME'
CHEETAH CONSERVATION FUND

The sleek and long-legged cheetah is losing its race for survival. Once a common animal found on five continents, the cheetah is now an endangered species. Loss of habitat, poaching, competition with large predators and ranchers, as well as its own loss of genetic variation, is killing off the remaining cheetahs. Unfortunately, captive breeding efforts have not proven meaningful to the cheetah's hopes of survival. The cheetah needs a large expanse of land to survive, but with the growth of the human population, this area is becoming smaller and smaller.

The largest population of cheetahs is in Namibia. Since the country's recent expansion, there was a drastic decline in cheetah numbers in the 1980s, when the population was halved in just 10 years, leaving an estimated total of fewer than 2,500 animals.

Now, only the 'human animal' can save the cheetah from extinction.

WHAT YOU CAN DO...

● Become a member of the Cheetah Conservation Fund (CCF). Visit the CCF website at www.cheetah.org. For more information, call +1 (513) 487 3899 in the US or +264 (0) 6730 6225 in Namibia.

● You can sponsor or adopt a cheetah cub or family, or simply make a donation to the CCF.

FACT BOX

COMMON NAME: Cheetah

SCIENTIFIC NAME: *Acinonyx jubatus*

STATUS: Protected species in Namibia. Endangered under the United States Endangered Species Act. Listed on CITES Appendix I. First listed on 1 July 1975.

POPULATION: About 12,400 cheetah remain in 25 African countries, and maybe 100-200 cats survive in Iran. Namibia has the world's largest number of cheetahs, yet only 3,000 remain in the wild.

LIFESPAN: Studies have not been conducted in the wild on longevity; eight to 12 years is average in captivity.

RANGE: Once found throughout Asia and Africa, the species is now only scattered in Iran and various countries in sub-Saharan Africa.

THREATS: Decline in prey, loss of habitat, poaching, and indiscriminate trapping and shooting as a livestock predator threaten the survival of the cheetah throughout its range.

CHIMPANZEE

'BEING KILLED FOR BUSHMEAT, OUR NEAREST RELATIVES ARE GOING TO DISAPPEAR FOR EVER IF WE CAN'T STOP POACHING AND HABITAT DESTRUCTION' PRO WILDLIFE

Chimps are the species most similar to humans – both genetically and behaviourally. However, increased encroachment of humans into their habitat and poaching threaten their survival. Whereas chimpanzees have always been hunted for consumption, the impact of hunting has become disastrous in recent years: growing human populations, combined with the opening up of formerly inaccessible areas (eg through logging companies or for road construction), have resulted in a massive and increasing hunt.

Chimps are especially sought after due to the relatively large amount of meat that a hunter can obtain with one single bullet. Furthermore, according to an old tradition, meat from great apes is supposed to be particularly healthy. Despite being protected legally, poaching has become a lucrative business and thousands of chimps are killed annually. Often, poachers kill all adults of a chimp group, whereas the surviving infants are sold as pets. Most of them suffer in chains or small cages.

FACT BOX

COMMON NAME: Chimpanzee, chimp

SCIENTIFIC NAME: *Pan troglodytes*

STATUS: Endangered

POPULATION: There are four subspecies: the western chimp (*P. t. verus*) with about 38,000 individuals; Nigeria chimp (*P. t. vellerosus*) 6,000; Central chimp (*P. t. troglodytes*) 93,000; and Eastern chimp (*P. t. schweinfurthii*) 98,000.

LIFESPAN: Up to 60 years.

RANGE: Chimps live in west and central Africa. The largest populations now exist in the Democratic Republic of Congo, Gabon and Cameroon.

THREATS: Populations have been decimated by more than two thirds within the last three decades. Chimpanzees are mainly threatened by poaching for the bushmeat trade and deforestation, but also by diseases and capture as pets and for research.

WHAT YOU CAN DO...

● Adopt a chimp (visit the website at www.prowildlife.de/en/adoption/adoption). The money raised helps PRO WILDLIFE to rescue primate orphans, run education programmes and fight habitat destruction and poaching.

● Write to the EU to halt timber imports from unsustainable logging: EU Environment Commissioner, Environment DG, European Commission, B-1049 Brussels, Belgium.

COCO-DE-MER

'TRADE IN THE COCO-DE-MER SEEDS IS NOW CLOSELY CONTROLLED, BUT POACHING REMAINS A PROBLEM BECAUSE OF THEIR HIGH VALUE ON THE TOURIST MARKET' **BOTANIC GARDENS CONSERVATION INTERNATIONAL**

Producing the largest seeds in the plant kingdom (weighing up to 30kg), this giant of the plant world was known to sailors in the Indian Ocean long before its real home was discovered. Over the ages, seeds of this legendary palm were found washed up on deserted beaches or floating on the waves and they become known as the 'coconuts of the sea' appearing to come from some mythical oceanic plant. Their suggestive two-lobed form gave rise to many legends, including a belief that they possessed aphrodisiac powers.

The true home of this mysterious plant is the Seychelles, where only two populations remain in the wild. Much prized, coco-de-mer seeds have commanded high prices for centuries. Trade in the seeds is now closely controlled, but poaching remains a problem because of their high value on the tourist market. Although protected within National Parks, the two remaining populations are nevertheless threatened by fire and encroachment by invasive plants.

WHAT YOU CAN DO...

● Coco-de-mer plants can be seen in various botanic gardens around the world. You can support the conservation activities of your local botanic garden in various ways. For some ideas, visit www.bgci.org/worldwide/get_involved.

● Find out more about the work of Botanic Gardens Conservation International, the world's largest network for plant conservation. Visit www.bgci.org or call +44 (0) 20 8332 5953.

FACT BOX

COMMON NAME: Coco-de-mer

SCIENTIFIC NAME: *Lodoicea maldivica*

STATUS: Vulnerable

POPULATION: Only two natural populations of this species remain. The long-term overexploitation of the seeds has virtually wiped out natural regeneration.

LIFESPAN: Coco-de-mer palms take 25-50 years to reach maturity and bear fruit. Fruit may take two years to germinate.

RANGE: Natural stands of the Coco-de-mer are found only on the islands of Praslin and Curieuse in the Seychelles. It is extinct on St Pierre, Chauve-Souris and Round Islands. Planted subpopulations occur on Mahé and Silhouette Islands. Individuals are also being cultivated in various botanic gardens around the world.

THREATS: The seeds are highly prized and their collection has virtually stopped all natural regeneration. Remaining populations are also threatened by fire and encroachment by invasive plants.

BGCI
Plants for the Planet

COMMON HIPPOPOTAMUS

'ONCE REGARDED AS WIDESPREAD, THE COMMON HIPPOPOTAMUS IS NOW AT RISK OF EXTINCTION DUE TO HABITAT LOSS, POACHING AND THE EFFECTS OF CLIMATE CHANGE' **FRIENDS OF CONSERVATION**

Charismatic and social animals, hippopotami or 'river horses' are gregarious creatures, found in African wetlands, swamps and rivers. Unfortunately, due to the growth in human population, hippo habitat – in common with that of many other species – is gradually being encroached upon. Changes to the climate mean that water courses are drying up, while a further major threat to the hippo population includes poaching, which has increased greatly since the elephant ivory ban a few years ago. Hippo teeth are sought after as an alternative, for example, in the manufacture of souvenirs.

Friends of Conservation (FOC) work in the Masai Mara region of Kenya with local communities to develop and promote a balance between their needs and those of wildlife. FOC is involved in and raises funds for wildlife monitoring and research, anti-poaching activities, habitat protection, carbon-reduction programmes and environmental education.

WHAT YOU CAN DO...

● By becoming a member of Friends of Conservation you can help support wildlife and habitat protection worldwide. The website at www.foc-uk.com has more information.

● When travelling, consider offsetting the carbon dioxide emissions which contribute to climate change by donating to FOC programmes which aim to mitigate these effects, such as reforestation or encouraging the use of alternative fuels. Use an online carbon calculator at www.foc-uk.com.

FACT BOX

COMMON NAME: Common hippopotamus

SCIENTIFIC NAME: *Hippopotamus amphibius*

STATUS: Vulnerable

POPULATION: Many of the subpopulation groups in west Africa contain fewer than 50 individuals, well below the minimum considered to be viable. Overall, the total population is estimated at around 125,000.

LIFESPAN: Males reach maturity between six to 14 years and females between seven to 15 years. Their lifespan is between 40-50 years.

RANGE: Found throughout Sub-Saharan Africa, but in decline. The largest current populations remain in the Nile River valley of east Africa.

THREATS: Loss of grazing land due to human settlement, the effects of climate change on habitat, and poaching for its meat, skins and ivory teeth.

COMMON SKATE

'WITH POPULATIONS DECLINING TO CRITICALLY ENDANGERED STATUS, THE COMMON SKATE SHOULD BE RENAMED THE UNCOMMON SKATE' THE SHARK TRUST

A close relative of sharks, common skate were once an abundant species in the fish communities of north-west Europe. The largest European rajid, the common skate has been targeted as food since the early twentieth century. These slow-growing, late-maturing animals have simply not been able to withstand targeted fisheries, and populations have all but disappeared from many coastal areas. Due to mankind's impact, the name common skate is now a misnomer.

There is no disputing the majesty of a common skate and the importance of maintaining them as an integral element of our marine biodiversity. Common skate are still targeted by fisheries that land small, immature skate with increased frequency. The Shark Trust is raising public awareness and campaigning for realistic protection for these creatures. If we can reduce the demand for skate products, then perhaps there will be a future for the common skate.

FACT BOX

COMMON NAME: Common skate

SCIENTIFIC NAME: *Dipturus batis*

STATUS: Critically endangered

POPULATION: Historically one of the most abundant rajids in the north-east Atlantic, the coastal populations are now restricted to a few refuge sites, the largest of these estimated at just 500 individuals.

LIFESPAN: If they survive to maturity, they can live for over 50 years.

RANGE: Formally common in the Mediterranean and north-east Atlantic, common skate have disappeared from most inshore areas and are now found sporadically across their range.

THREATS: Continued fishing pressure.

WHAT YOU CAN DO...

• Join the Great Eggcase Hunt and help the Shark Trust learn more about the distribution of all skates and rays. Visit www.sharktrust.org/eggcase for eggcase information and resources.

• Find out more about the only UK charity dedicated to the conservation of sharks, skates and rays. Visit the Shark Trust at www.sharktrust.org or call +44 (0) 1752 672008.

CORNCOCKLE

'MODERN HERBICIDE USE HAS DRIVEN THIS ONCE WIDESPREAD CORNFIELD FLOWER TO NEAR EXTINCTION IN THE UK' PLANTLIFE INTERNATIONAL

The story of the corncockle is the story of arable farming in Britain. Attractive and unmistakable, its single flowers of a deep pink colour have been present in our arable fields since the Iron Age. Corncockle was once common as part of species-rich cornfield communities.

However, along with other threatened, arable flowers such as the cornflower, it now faces extinction. Apart from occasional appearances after deep-buried seed is brought to the surface, the corncockle is now rarely seen in arable fields. Its downfall came about because its large, black seeds taste so bitter. This meant that when the corn and rye crops were milled for flour, the resulting bread was inedible. The development of seed-cleaning technologies at the end of the nineteenth century and the application of modern herbicides in the twentieth sealed its fate and our countryside has lost, perhaps forever, the tall, bright flowers with their delicate, purple-streaked petals.

FACT BOX

COMMON NAME: Corncockle

SCIENTIFIC NAME: *Agrostemma githago*

STATUS: On 'waiting list' for the Vascular Plant Red Data List for GB

POPULATION: Although widespread as an introduction, there are only one or two sites where it survives as an original, ancient cornfield plant.

LIFESPAN: An annual species so dies at the end of the season. However, its buried seeds can remain dormant for a long time.

RANGE: Native range uncertain, perhaps eastern Mediterranean; spread with cultivation throughout temperate and southern Europe, and other areas.

THREATS: Modern farming practices, particularly seed-cleaning processes and the application of herbicide and fertiliser on arable land.

WHAT YOU CAN DO...

• Adopt a flower (visit the website www.plantlife.org.uk). The money raised supports Plantlife's work to rescue wild plants on the brink of extinction and to conserve sites of exceptional botanical importance.

• Be aware that corncockle seeds found in commercial wildflower seed mixes are not sourced from the UK and the resulting plants will have a different genetic identity. Enjoy them in your garden but do not scatter these seeds into the wider countryside!

PLANTLIFE

CUVIER'S BEAKED WHALE

'EVEN IN THEIR REMOTE HABITATS, THESE WHALES ARE NOT SAFE FROM THE THREATS POSED BY HUMANS' ORCA

This species is just one in a family of 21 beaked whale species. Cuvier's beaked whales are one of the better-known of these mysterious whales, yet we know virtually nothing compared to other whales and dolphins. We know so little because these animals spend most of their time diving to depths of 1,000m or more and spending long periods beneath the surface. At depth, they feed mainly on squid, which they seek out in the darkness using echolocation clicks.

Yet even in their remote habitats, they are not safe from the threats posed by humans. Military sonar is particularly harmful to Cuvier's and other beaked whales and has been associated with numerous mass strandings over the last decade. Plastic debris in the ocean also finds its way into the stomachs of whales and dolphins when it's ingested accidentally and this is a problem for Cuvier's beaked whales. This species is also caught or entangled in fishing nets and is cause for conservation concern in some areas.

WHAT YOU CAN DO...

• Many beaked whales found dead in recent years have had large quantities of plastic bags and other rubbish in their stomachs – something we can all help with by cutting down on plastic consumption, and being more responsible towards waste disposal.

• Find out more and support the work of Organisation Cetacea, by visiting www.orcaweb.org.uk and the Beaked Whale Resource www.beakedwhaleresource.com.

FACT BOX

COMMON NAME: Cuvier's beaked whale

SCIENTIFIC NAME: *Ziphius cavirostris*

STATUS: Data deficient

POPULATION: Because Cuvier's beaked whales are seldom seen during at-sea surveys, it is extremely difficult to estimate population sizes. A minimum population estimate of 20,000 individuals is available for the eastern Tropical Pacific and tens of individuals have been identified in local areas. No estimates of global population are available.

LIFESPAN: They are long-lived animals, and it is thought that their lifespan is at least 25 years.

RANGE: A widespread distribution across the Atlantic, Pacific and Indian Oceans. They prefer deep-water areas.

THREATS: Noise pollution, ocean debris and entanglement in fishing nets.

FOR THE OCEAN GOING NATURALIST

DALL'S PORPOISE

'SINCE 1980 NEARLY 400,000 DALL'S PORPOISES HAVE BEEN KILLED IN JAPAN IN WHAT IS NOW THE WORLD'S LARGEST CETACEAN HUNT' ENVIRONMENTAL INVESTIGATION AGENCY

The international moratorium on commercial whaling, implemented in 1986, saved the great whales from extinction. It did not, however, protect smaller cetaceans and one stocky little black and white porpoise still suffers an appalling annual slaughter. The Dall's porpoise is an energetic swimmer. Capable of speeds up to 55km/h, it is the only porpoise frequently observed riding the bow-waves of ships. It used to be common around Japan, but since 1980, nearly 400,000 have been killed there in the world's largest cetacean hunt. Chasing a dangerously high annual quota of 17,700, Japanese hunters increasingly target nursing females because they travel slowly to protect their calves and are easier to kill. The calves are left to starve and the loss of females upsets the sex ratio in this population, which is now at risk. The Scientific Committee of the International Whaling Commission (IWC) has expressed 'extreme concern' over this 'clearly unsustainable' hunt, yet Japan wants to restore commercial killing of all the world's whales.

WHAT YOU CAN DO...

• The Environmental Investigation Agency's (EIA) ongoing investigations and campaigning have been a persuasive influence at the IWC. Support EIA's Dall's Porpoise Appeal by making a donation. Log on to www.eia-international.org or call +44 (0) 20 7354 7960.

• Join EIA by becoming a member and receive our twice-yearly newsletter, *Investigator*, as well as access to a wide range of videos and reports at special low members' rates. Log on to www.eia-international.org or call +44 (0) 20 7354 7960 to find out more.

DELHI SANDS FLOWER-LOVING FLY

'THE DELHI SANDS FLOWER-LOVING FLY IS A FLAGSHIP FOR THE WHOLE DELHI SANDS ECOSYSTEM. AS LONG AS THE FLY STAYS AFLOAT, THE REST OF ITS HABITAT DOES, TOO' XERCES SOCIETY

The Delhi Sands flower-loving fly is a giant in the fly world. It is more than an inch long, with beautiful green eyes and a craving for nectar. It also is native to the irreplaceable – and rapidly disappearing – Delhi Sands ecosystem in southern California. Because of urban development, researchers estimate only 2-3% of the fly's sand dune habitat remains.

Scientists have called the Delhi Sands flower-loving fly a flagship species for the whole Delhi Sands ecosystem. Protecting the Delhi fly's habitat will preserve important open space that is habitat to a variety of wildlife. We may not know what specific role the Delhi fly plays in these dunes, but, as the ecologist Aldo Leopold said: 'To keep every cog and wheel is the first precaution of intelligent tinkering.' We must act now if we are to save the Delhi Sands flower-loving fly – our unique natural heritage – from vanishing for ever.

WHAT YOU CAN DO...

● Contact the US Fish and Wildlife Service and ask that they prioritise protection of the Delhi Sands flower-loving fly's ecosystem. US Fish and Wildlife Service, Carlsbad Fish and Wildlife Office, 2730 Loker Ave. West, Carlsbad, CA 92008.

● Join the Xerces Society for Invertebrate Conservation and help us to protect the Delhi Sands flower-loving fly and other invertebrates at www.xerces.org or call +1 (503) 232 6639.

FACT BOX

COMMON NAME: Delhi Sands flower-loving fly

SCIENTIFIC NAME: *Rhaphiomidas terminatus abdominalis*

STATUS: Critically imperilled; endangered

POPULATION: The Delhi fly is only known from 12 sites and less than 3% of its habitat remains.

LIFESPAN: Adults live two to three weeks. Larvae may be picked up by ants and taken to the ant nest where they are fed and tended as ant brood and live throughout the rest of the year.

RANGE: Can only be found in the Delhi Sands ecosystem in southern California, USA.

THREATS: Development of the Delhi Sands flower-loving fly's habitat for housing developments, roads and shopping malls.

THE XERCES SOCIETY FOR INVERTEBRATE CONSERVATION

DRILL

'RELATIVELY UNKNOWN, DRILLS ARE CURRENTLY THE HIGHEST PRIORITY AFRICAN PRIMATE FOR CONSERVATION.' *ACF*

The drill, an endangered forest-dwelling baboon, lives in the rainforests of Western Cameroon, Nigeria and Bioko Island. Drills prefer primary undisturbed forests and are rarely seen in open country, away from the shelter of trees.

Male drills can be distinguished from male mandrills, their close relations, by the absence of a brightly red and blue facial skin.

Little is known about the ecology or behaviour of drills in the wild, but we do know that the conservation status of this species is precarious due to human pressure. Forest destruction and fragmentation throughout its highly restricted range is causing local extinction of the species, and of other primates. These areas are also centres of high endemism – many of these species are not found anywhere else.

In addition, drills are hunted extensively for their meat, which is being sold at local markets.

FACT BOX

COMMON NAME: Drill

SCIENTIFIC NAME: *Mandrillus leucophaeus*

STATUS: Endangered

POPULATION: Exact numbers unknown; the remaining population is estimated to be as small as 3,000 individuals.

LIFESPAN: Drills in captivity can live up to 45 years, but their lifespan in the wild is unknown.

RANGE: Lowland, coastal and montane rainforests (up to 1,000m) of western Cameroon, Nigeria and Bioko Island (Equatorial Guinea).

THREATS: Habitat loss and fragmentation due to deforestation as well as hunting for the bushmeat trade.

The African Conservation Foundation

EASTERN LOWLAND GORILLA

'WHILE FACTIONS IN D.R. CONGO FIGHT FOR SUPREMACY AND MINERAL RESOURCES, THE WORLD'S ONLY EASTERN LOWLAND GORILLAS FIGHT FOR THEIR SURVIVAL' THE GORILLA ORGANIZATION

Gorillas are one of our closest living relatives, and their normally placid, pensive disposition has rightly earned them the nickname of gentle giants. However, human actions have taken almost all populations of gorillas to the brink of extinction.

The mountain gorilla has one of the smallest populations, but the encouraging news is that this has been increasing in recent years. Meanwhile, the neighbouring population of eastern lowland gorillas has suffered an 80-90% decline since 2000 and we are all to blame in some way. The rapid growth of micro-technologies, from mobile phones to laptop computers, led to an enormous demand for the metal tantalum, used in capacitors. Deposits of tantalum, as well as tin, are found under the gorilla habitat and opportunistic miners have degraded the environment and hunted the gorillas. Their habitat is also still under the control of rebel militias, and their survival hangs in the balance.

WHAT YOU CAN DO...

• Find out more about the issues and support the work of The Gorilla Organization (formerly the Dian Fossey Gorilla Fund) at www.gorillas.org and www.durbanprocess.net.

• Lobby companies to join The Gorilla Organization's 'gorilla-friendly' technology scheme and send your old mobile phones to The Gorilla Organization for recycling.

FACT BOX

COMMON NAME: Eastern lowland gorilla (Grauer's gorilla)

SCIENTIFIC NAME: *Gorilla beringei graueri*

STATUS: Endangered

POPULATION: A census conducted in 1998 suggested there were approximately 17,000 eastern lowland gorillas. Since then the population has been decimated, and while it has not been possible to get a reliable estimate of the population size, at present it is thought that only around 2,000-3,000 gorillas survive.

LIFESPAN: Gorillas in the wild can live for between 30-35 years.

RANGE: The eastern lowland gorilla is confined to the eastern provinces of the Democratic Republic of Congo.

THREATS: Hunting and degradation of their habitat.

the gorilla organization

ENGLISH ELM

'INFECTION OF HEALTHY TREES IS POSSIBLE AT ANY TIME'
THE TREE COUNCIL

The English elm was once a common sight in the landscape, planted as part of hedges and land enclosures in the eighteenth century and subsequently in parks and streets across the UK. Immature trees remain a common feature in hedgerows as the elm forms suckers that produce new trees.

It is this homogeneity of genetic stock that makes the elm more susceptible to the Dutch elm disease fungus (*Ophiostoma novo-ulmi*) that killed more than 15,000,000 UK trees at the time of the initial disease outbreak in 1967, and continues to add to the toll. In addition, mature trees in public locations are often subject to vandalism and saplings are often destroyed; inappropriate hedgerow management may also lead to the loss of naturally regenerating elms.

English elms do not readily regenerate from seeds in Britain but have the ability to regenerate by vegetative means. There is a low base population and the survival of the species depends on planting.

WHAT YOU CAN DO...

● Be a volunteer Tree Warden – contact The Tree Council (www.treecouncil.org.uk) at: 71 Newcomen Street, London SE1 1YT, +44 (0) 20 7407 9992, or info@treecouncil.org.uk.
● Let your local Biodiversity Partnership, Tree Warden or tree officer know if you have an elm on your land, so that information on the last surviving mature elm trees and elm sucker recovery growth can be gathered and monitored.

FACT BOX

COMMON NAME: English elm

SCIENTIFIC NAME: *Ulmus minor*

STATUS: Vulnerable

POPULATION: Estimated at around 40,000 mature elms.

LIFESPAN: Elm bark beetles breed in freshly dead elms; the new beetles emerge from breeding sites and search for living elms, where they feed in the small twig crotches high in the tree canopy, chewing into young shoots. As they do so, spores of the pathogen may be brushed off and transferred to the open wound in the tree, from where it is carried through the tree, resulting in the infection that kills. Where recently dead elms stand, the breeding grounds exist for the cycle to continue.

RANGE: Across the UK.

THREATS: *Ophiostoma novo-ulmi* – a yeast-like fungus spread by elm bark beetles – is estimated to have killed more than 80% of the UK elm population and continues unabated.

THE TREE COUNCIL

ETHIOPIAN WOLF

'TRAPPED IN THEIR HIGHLAND HAVENS, ETHIOPIAN WOLVES PERCH ON THE EDGE OF SURVIVAL IN EVER-SHRINKING HABITATS, AT THE MERCY OF DISEASE AND PERSECUTION' WildCRU

These elegant, long-legged wolves are found only in a handful of mountain pockets in Ethiopia, living in family groups with a fascinating network of social relationships and hierarchies. Because they are specialised to predate on high-altitude rodents, only some 500 survive today in these highland relicts, surrounded by expanding agriculture and threatened by disease and persecution.

The Ethiopian Wolf Conservation Programme (EWCP) has been working to reduce the most urgent threats to their survival. It monitors packs continuously, vaccinates domestic dogs – the reservoir of deadly diseases – and raises awareness among children, adults and institutions, of the plight of the wolves and the need to preserve the mountains' natural resources needed by people nearby and further down the slopes.

EWCP promotes these charismatic creatures as a flagship for the protection of a rich array of endemic fauna and flora in the highlands of Ethiopia.

WHAT YOU CAN DO...

• Find out more and donate to the EWCP by visiting www.ethiopianwolf.org or calling WildCRU at +44 (0) 1865 393100. You can also adopt an Ethiopian wolf pack through the Born Free Foundation, which can be visited at www.bornfree.org.uk.

• To learn more about the work of Oxford University's WildCRU to protect endangered wildlife, visit www.wildcru.org.

FACT BOX

COMMON NAME: Ethiopian wolf

SCIENTIFIC NAME: *Canis simensis*

STATUS: Endangered

POPULATION: Five hundred adults, scattered in seven mountain ranges, which arguably makes them the rarest canid in the world. The largest population is found in the Bale Mountains National Park.

LIFESPAN: Up to 13 years in the wild. There are no Ethiopian wolves in captivity.

RANGE: Found only in a handful of Ethiopia's mountain peaks over 3,000m above sea level, with grasslands and meadows where their rodent prey thrives.

THREATS: Rabies and canine distemper transmitted by the domestic dogs of mountain shepherds. Loss of Afroalpine habitat to subsistence agriculture and grazing.

WILD CRU
WILDLIFE CONSERVATION RESEARCH UNIT

EURASIAN LYNX

'BY THE END OF THE NINETEENTH CENTURY, IN MOST PARTS OF EUROPE, THE LYNX HAD VANISHED FROM EXISTENCE' PRO NATURA

One hardly ever sees him: the Eurasian lynx. And not only because few survive. This tuft-eared wildcat is quite shy, living in forests where he can hide himself well and is mostly active at dusk.

The lynx hunts small cloven-footed animals which he can sneak up on masterfully. His most important prey in Switzerland are deer and chamois.

By the end of the nineteenth century, in most parts of Europe, as in Switzerland, the lynx vanished from existence. Deforestation, a massive decrease of its natural prey, and hunting were to blame.

For a long time, Pro Natura has struggled to bring back the lynx. In 1971, the first lynx was reintroduced to Switzerland and Pro Natura has vigorously supported the species ever since.

But once again, the 'alp tiger' must fight for pure survival in its original habitat.

FACT BOX

COMMON NAME: Eurasian lynx

SCIENTIFIC NAME: *Lynx lynx*

STATUS: Near threatened

POPULATION: Less than 50,000 (worldwide); approximately 100 in Switzerland.

LIFESPAN: The lynx reaches an age of approximately 16 years.

RANGE: Found in the forests of Europe and Asia (north of the Himalayas).

THREATS: Destruction of its habitat (deforestation), the decrease of its natural prey, hunting, a change in the natural dynamic between species.

WHAT YOU CAN DO...

• Become a member of the nature conservation organisation Pro Natura, or support our species protection effort by making a donation at www.pronatura.ch (or by telephone at +41 (61) 317 9191).

• Information about the Eurasian lynx, and the specific needs for its environment, can be found at www.pronatura.ch and www.kora.ch.

EUROPEAN STAG BEETLE

'THE LOSS OF THE STAG BEETLE WOULD MEAN THE LOSS OF THE LARGEST AND MOST STRIKING LAND BEETLE IN BRITAIN. WE MUST ACT NOW TO CONSERVE THIS BEAUTIFUL INSECT' PTES

With their shiny chestnut-brown wing cases (head and thorax black) and huge antler-like jaws, the stag beetle is a top contender for Britain's most impressive invertebrate. They are almost prehistoric in appearance, and are particularly dramatic when in flight on still summer evenings.

Once common across western Europe, the stag beetle is becoming increasingly rare in many countries, and so it is vital that we work to conserve them in the UK, where more of them survive. The species depends on undisturbed decaying dead wood habitat. The female burrows down and lays her eggs near the rotting wood. These hatch into larvae, which feed on the supply of dead wood, taking up to seven years to develop into adults. In adult form, stag beetles usually live for a couple of months, searching for mates so that the cycle can continue. In addition to habitat loss, stag beetles fall victim to cats, magpies, road traffic and often drown in water butts.

WHAT YOU CAN DO...

• Why not become a stag beetle-friendly gardener? Try creating a log pile in a quiet, shady area and avoid using insecticides in the garden.

• For more information on stag beetles, visit www.ptes.org. To take part in one of PTES' national stag beetle monitoring surveys go to www.greatstaghunt.org or call +44 (0) 20 7498 4533.

FACT BOX

COMMON NAME: European stag beetle

SCIENTIFIC NAME: *Lucanus cervus*

STATUS: Protected

POPULATION: The exact population figures for the stag beetle are not known. They are in serious decline on mainland Europe and here in the UK their numbers are also decreasing, with concerns that they may soon disappear from the peripheral areas of their range.

LIFESPAN: Larvae take up to seven years to develop into adults. Their lives are short, at around four to eight weeks.

RANGE: South-east England and western Europe.

THREATS: Many are killed by cats and magpies, or drowned in ponds and water butts. The larval form is very susceptible to predation, and loss of undisturbed habitat may be resulting in a shortage of egg laying sites.

PEOPLE'S TRUST
FOR ENDANGERED SPECIES

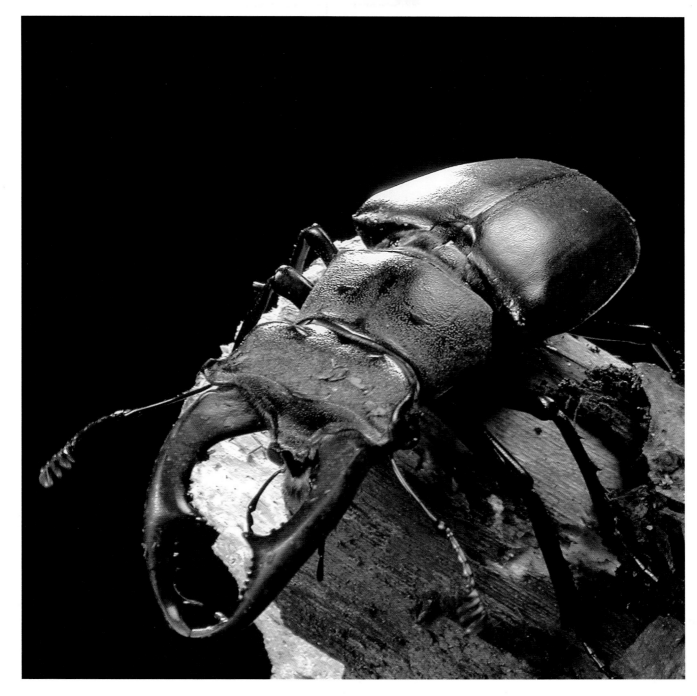

GIANT PANDA

'DESPITE BEING UNIVERSALLY LOVED AND THE SYMBOL OF A NATION, THE GIANT PANDA'S FUTURE REMAINS UNCERTAIN' WWF

Peaceful and mostly vegetarian, giant pandas have steadily lost their forest habitat to China's expanding human population. These striking animals are now confined to fragmented forest patches high in the mountains of south-western China. These same mountains form the watershed for China's Yangtze and Yellow Rivers, whose basins are the economic heart of China and home to over 500 million people. As China's economy continues its rapid development, it is now more important than ever to conserve the forest home of the giant panda – not just to safeguard this well-loved species, but to maintain the subsistence fisheries, agriculture, and water resources essential for nearly 40% of China's people.

A member of the bear family, the giant panda is the only species in its genus. The animals have the digestive system of a carnivore, but have adapted to a vegetarian diet, and depend almost exclusively on bamboo as a food source.

WHAT YOU CAN DO...

● Log on to www.passport.panda.org to find out how you can take action to help protect this and other species and fragile environments.

● Support the work of the World Wildlife Federation in your country and abroad. For more information, visit www.panda.org.

GOLDEN CONURE

'WITH 50 MILLION PARROTS IN CAPTIVITY, AND OVER 100 SPECIES THREATENED IN THE WILD, THERE IS A LOT OF WORK TO DO' WORLD PARROT TRUST

Parrots are beautiful, charismatic and have the ability to talk, but sadly this puts them in increased danger of extinction. As with many other species, habitat loss and introduced predators are big problems, but parrots also face capture in large numbers for the pet trade.

Their dazzling plumage has made golden conures much sought after as pet and aviary birds. They come from an area of conflict between farmers, ranchers and poor peasants, plus illegal logging and controversy over dams and mining all put their habitat at risk.

Until 1990 little was known about golden conure populations, feeding or nesting habits, but initial projects show that they often live in family 'clans' and roost together in tree cavities at night, making them easy to trap. Enforcing laws and further research in Brazil are needed to help this species survive. Education in local schools is underway including a poster encouraging reporting of trapping.

FACT BOX

COMMON NAME: Golden conure

SCIENTIFIC NAME: *Guaruba guarouba*

STATUS: CITES Appendix 1. Endangered.

POPULATION: Estimate of 2,500 in the wild and 1,500 in captivity.

LIFESPAN: Possibly 35-40 years

RANGE: Brazil

THREATS: This species suffers from the destruction of its rainforest habitat, illegal trapping and hunting for food.

WHAT YOU CAN DO...

● Support work for golden conures by buying a 'Golden Conure Fund' T-shirt, or a print of an original painting by Grant Hacking.

● To help parrot conservation and to find out more about how to keep your pet parrot happy and healthy, join the World Parrot Trust. Visit the website www.worldparrottrust.org or call on +44 (0) 1736 751026.

GOULDIAN FINCH

'SAVING THE GOULDIAN FINCH REQUIRES URGENT, SWEEPING CHANGES TO LAND MANAGEMENT IN AUSTRALIA'S TROPICAL SAVANNAS' AUSTRALIAN WILDLIFE CONSERVANCY

The multi-coloured Gouldian finch is endemic to the tropical savannas of northern Australia. Once found in dazzling flocks of thousands, in recent decades they have dwindled dramatically. The entire population now numbers less than 2,500 adult birds.

The reasons for this precipitous decline are speculative, but almost certainly revolve around the change during the last century from Aboriginal land management to one geared towards pastoral production. Grazing by cattle, and a radical shift in fire patterns towards more extensive and frequent fires, have affected seed production in the grass species that Gouldians rely on for food. Many other bird species that eat grass seed have shown similar patterns of decline. Saving the Gouldian and other threatened species of the tropical savannas requires a concerted effort by government and non-government conservation agencies and landowners (including pastoralists and Aboriginal communities) to manage fire and cattle across huge areas of northern Australia.

FACT BOX

COMMON NAME: Gouldian finch

SCIENTIFIC NAME: *Erythrura gouldiae*

STATUS: Endangered C2a(ii)

POPULATION: Fewer than 2,500 adults

LIFESPAN: Poor data, but probably one to two years in the wild, and up to four years in captivity.

RANGE: Previously across Australia's tropical savannas from Queensland, through the Northern Territory, to Western Australia. Reduced now to isolated populations, mainly in Western Australia and the Northern Territory, with only sporadic sightings of very small numbers of birds from Queensland.

THREATS: Changed fire patterns, grazing by cattle.

WHAT YOU CAN DO...

• Support the Australian Wildlife Conservancy (www.australianwildlife.org), a non-governmental organisation (NGO) dedicated to saving Australia's threatened wildlife and ecosystems.

• Pay a visit to Mornington Wildlife Sanctuary (www.australianwildlife. org.au/mornington4.asp) to see Gouldian finches in the wild, and to learn about the Australian Wildlife Conservancy's work on Mornington and also at its other sanctuaries throughout Australia.

australian
wildlife
conservancy

GRAND CAYMAN BLUE IGUANA

'PROBABLY THE MOST MAGNIFICENT, BUT YET THE MOST CRITICALLY ENDANGERED OF ALL IGUANAS, THE GRAND CAYMAN BLUE CAN STILL BE SAVED' INTERNATIONAL REPTILE CONSERVATION FOUNDATION

Imagine living blue dragons, with fascinating personalities and complex social lives not unlike our own.

Not quite the first thing you would expect from a lizard. Once Grand Cayman's largest land animal, the only threat adult blue iguanas had to deal with was competition from other blue iguanas.

With humans and their furry companions on the scene, rats and feral cats now attack and kill young blue iguanas, while roaming dogs kill adult iguanas, including nesting females.

Escalating loss of their habitats to human settlement, and road kills have added to the blue iguana's woes, and by the turn of this century they had declined to the point of functional extinction.

Only just in time, local and international conservation workers launched the Blue Iguana Recovery Program, which in a remarkably successful, groundbreaking effort is beginning to bring the blues back from the brink.

WHAT YOU CAN DO...

● Sponsor a real blue iguana (visit www.blueiguana.ky). All sponsorship and other donations – from the smallest private contribution to much-needed major grants – go to the Blue Iguana Recovery Program, an internationally acclaimed conservation effort.

● Join the International Reptile Conservation Foundation, receive the journal *Iguana*, and help support this and other significant reptile conservation efforts (www.ircf.org).

FACT BOX

COMMON NAME: Grand Cayman blue iguana

SCIENTIFIC NAME: *Cyclura lewisi*

STATUS: Critically endangered

POPULATION: In 2002, the wild population was between 10 and 25 individuals, with little or no survival of young to breeding age. Conservation workers have now restored about 120 young blues into protected areas.

LIFESPAN: Blue iguanas can probably live as long as humans. The oldest recorded was a captive which died aged 67.

RANGE: Blue iguanas are unique to the island of Grand Cayman, in the Cayman Islands.

THREATS: Habitat loss, predation by roaming dogs, feral cats and rats, road kills, illegal capture, and the genetic consequences of a very small population size.

IRCF

GREAT BARRIER REEF

'CORAL REEFS ARE THE OCEANS' ENGINES OF BIODIVERSITY – THE HOME OR NURSERY TO OVER A QUARTER OF THE KNOWN SPECIES OF MARINE FISH' THE CORAL REEF ALLIANCE

Stretching 2,300km in length and covering more than 300,000sq.km – so enormous it is visible from space – Australia's Great Barrier Reef is the largest tropical reef system in the world. Made up of more than 3,000 reefs, islands and coral cays, it is representative of the extraordinary beauty and richness of tropical coral reefs the world over. The reef's amazing diversity of species are so intricately interconnected that some scientists have referred to the Great Barrier Reef as a superorganism.

As with all coral reefs, it is sensitive to changes in climate, ocean currents, and to human activities. Despite its protected status, the reef is suffering the impacts of increasing sea temperature, coastal development, and additional nutrients running off land from agriculture and development.

If unchecked, we stand to lose not only a giant living system that has been thriving since the last ice age, but also the incalculable benefits we derive from its existence.

WHAT YOU CAN DO...

• Consume wisely. Small changes in what you buy can be a big help in conserving coral reefs. Avoid buying products made from sea turtles, sea stars, or coral. Most importantly, only purchase sustainably caught seafood.

• Join The Coral Reef Alliance and be part of the solution to protect coral reefs. The Coral Reef Alliance, 417 Montgomery Street, Suite 205, San Francisco, CA 94104. Call +1 (415) 834 0900, or visit www.coral.org.

FACT BOX

COMMON NAME: Great Barrier Reef

DESCRIPTION: Complex of fringing reefs, coral cays, and continental islands

STATUS: Endangered

SIZE: The Great Barrier Reef Marine Park was established in 1975, and it is the largest marine protected area in the world. It is approximately 348,700sq.km

POPULATION: It contains 1,500 species of fish, 400 species of corals, 4,000 species of molluscs, 500 species of seaweed, 215 species of birds, 16 species of sea snake, six species of turtle.

LIFESPAN: Over 1.5 million years old, the Great Barrier Reef is among the oldest ecosystems on the planet.

RANGE: East coast of Australia running from Bundaberg to the tip of the Cape York Peninsula.

THREATS: Bleaching due to climate change, run-off of fertiliser and pesticides from agricultural lands, and overfishing.

CORAL
THE CORAL REEF ALLIANCE

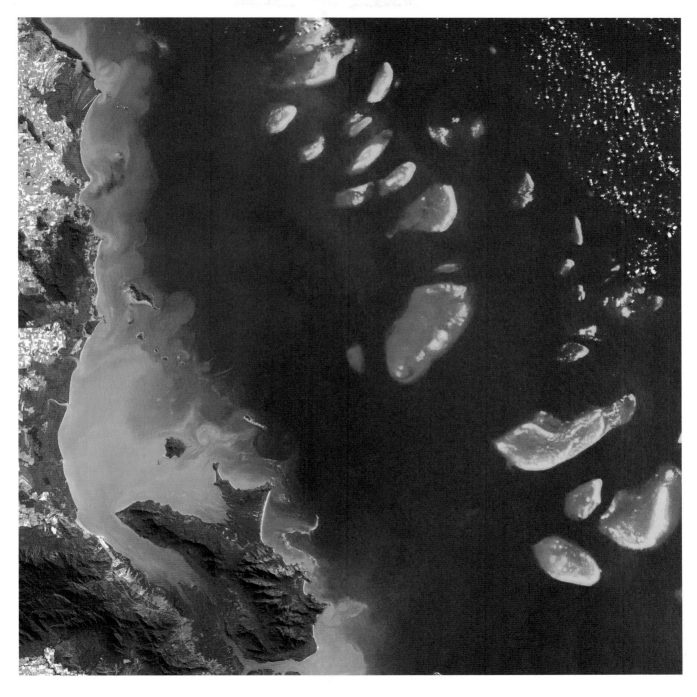

GREAT CRESTED NEWT

'WITH SO MANY THREATS TO FACE, IT IS EASY TO SEE WHY THE GREAT CRESTED NEWT IS SO VULNERABLE TO RAPID DECLINES' FROGLIFE

Great crested newts are the most easily recognised species of newt in Britain because of their size and colouring. Males exhibit a large crest during the breeding season and the white flashes on the tail distinguish them from the females. They have striking orange undersides with irregular black spots, and each pattern is unique to that individual.

Great crested newts, although widespread throughout much of Britain, are vulnerable to rapid loss and decline. The British population is amongst the largest in Europe, where they are threatened in several countries. The main threats to great crested newts range from loss of suitable breeding ponds, caused by water table reduction and ponds being filled in for site development, to agrochemicals leaching into ponds and the stocking of newt ponds with fish. Finally, terrestrial habitat destruction and fragmentation complete the long list.

FACT BOX

COMMON NAME: Great crested newt

SCIENTIFIC NAME: *Triturus cristatus*

STATUS: Least concern

POPULATION: The exact population number is not known, but there are believed to be around 360,000 in 18,000 ponds in Britain.

LIFESPAN: Long-lived, up to 14 years

RANGE: Great Britain, western, central and eastern Europe north of the Alps up to central Scandinavia and southern Finland. Usually found below 1,100m.

THREATS: Deliberate filling in or destruction of ponds, pond loss through natural succession, introduction of fish, chemical pollution and nutrification of breeding sites, loss of terrestrial habitat, habitat fragmentation, poor habitat management and pond deterioration through neglect.

WHAT YOU CAN DO...

● Become a Froglife Friend (visit www.froglife.org). The donations go towards various projects to help conserve native reptiles and amphibians.

● Find out more about Froglife's work by visiting www.froglife.org or by calling +44 (0) 1773 558444.

FROG*life*

GREEN TURTLE

'HUMAN-RELATED CAUSES ARE THE TOP CONTRIBUTOR TO THE DRASTIC DECLINES IN GREEN SEA TURTLE POPULATIONS. WE MUST BECOME MORE AWARE OF OUR IMPACT ON THEIR EXISTENCE'
WIMARCS

Green sea turtles are the largest of all the hard-shelled sea turtles, measuring over 100cm in carapace length and weighing on average 150km. Named for the colour of their fat, adult green turtles are herbivores and feed near-shore on seagrasses and algae.

Since green turtles are often found close to shore, local harvesting, coastal development and pollution have a severe impact on this species. The high incidence of fibropapillomas, or cancer-like tumours, in coastal areas has led scientists to suspect that marine pollution may be involved in the development and transfer of this disease. Little is known about fibropapilloma, although it is believed that a virus causes the fatal, lobed tumours that may cover the skin, eyes and internal organs of this species. Its occurrence has reached epidemic proportions in many populations, severely threatening the health, vitality and future of this charismatic species. Comprehensive research, conservation and education efforts are needed to ensure the survival of green turtles.

FACT BOX

COMMON NAME: Green turtle

SCIENTIFIC NAME: *Chelonia mydas*

STATUS: Endangered globally, with a continuing population decline.

POPULATION: Currently, it is estimated that approximately 88,000 adult female green turtles are nesting worldwide.

LIFESPAN: Unknown; the lifespan of the green turtle is estimated at up to 80 years.

RANGE: May be found in the warm waters of tropical and subtropical oceans worldwide.

THREATS: Fibropapilloma tumours, over-exploitation for meat, shell and eggs, loss of nesting and foraging habitat due to coastal development, incidental catch in fishing gear.

WHAT YOU CAN DO...

● Make a tax-deductible contribution to the West Indies Marine Animal Research and Conservation Service (WIMARCS). Your contribution will support vital research to better understand fibropapilloma, habitat utilisation and human impacts on foraging grounds. See www.wimarcs.org.

● Whether you live on or near a nesting beach, coastal waters, or you are holidaying in an area turtles live in, you can do your part. Don't drive vehicles, ride horses or allow dogs to dig on beaches during the nesting season.

GREVY'S ZEBRA

'GREVY'S ZEBRA NUMBERS UNDERWENT A DRAMATIC DECLINE IN THE 1970S DUE TO THE FUR TRADE. NOW IT COMPETES WITH DOMESTIC CATTLE FOR GRAZING AND WATER TO SURVIVE'
EARTHWATCH INSTITUTE

The superb, narrow striped coat of this, the largest of all wild horses, led to its dramatic decline in the 1970s when it became prized in the fur trade as a fashion item. Although poaching ceased some 20 years ago, the population has not subsequently recovered. Current research indicates that the competition with domestic cattle herds for grazing and water may be part of the problem. However, even in areas of Kenya where livestock do not occur, there is still a downward population trend. The likely reasons are competition with the numerous plains zebra and other wildlife, predation and disease.

Management to recover this species can only be put in place when there is a full understanding of the factors causing decline. An Earthwatch research project is designed to do just this and will focus on the behaviour of the species in relation to lions and how the zebra feed and drink – both in the presence and absence of domestic livestock.

FACT BOX

COMMON NAME: Grevy's zebra

SCIENTIFIC NAME: *Equus grevyi*

STATUS: Endangered

POPULATION: Grevy's zebra numbers are declining. Twenty-five years ago about 15,000 were found in Kenya, but now only about 2,000 remain. There are also 120-250 living in three isolated populations in Ethiopia.

LIFESPAN: About 10-25 years in the wild and up to 40 years in captivity.

RANGE: Found in north-eastern Kenya and Ethiopia. Formerly more widespread in both countries and occurred in Somalia, too.

THREATS: Poaching for the fur trade led to a dramatic decline in the 1970s. Although illegal hunting has ceased, competition with domestic stock for water and grazing areas remains a threat to its survival.

WHAT YOU CAN DO...

● Join the Earthwatch Grevy's zebra project in Kenya's Samburu area and help scientists determine how to save this species. Visit www.earthwatch.org for more information.

● The Saint Louis Zoo and its partners are working hard to protect the Grevy's zebra. You can help, too. Visit www.stlzoo.org/wildcareinstitute/grevyszebrasinthehornofafr/conservingthegrevyszebrain.

EARTHWATCH®
INSTITUTE

GREY NURSE SHARK

'URGENT ACTION IS NEEDED TO PROTECT THIS SHARK'
AUSTRALIAN MARINE CONSERVATION SOCIETY

A short history of the grey nurse shark paints a tale of mistaken identity and gross overfishing. Thousands of grey nurse sharks were killed during the 1960s and 1970s along the east Australian coastline because of their ferocious appearance and undeserved reputation as a 'man eater'. The grey nurse shark, however, is completely harmless and has become a favourite among divers who view these charismatic animals in their underwater critical habitats where they spend most of their time.

Incidental and illegal fishing continues to deplete this species, and today fewer than 500 individuals remain along the east Australian coastline. Urgent action is needed to protect the grey nurse shark, its habitat and food from all forms of fishing, particularly at the known critical habitat sites along the east Australian coastline.

WHAT YOU CAN DO...

• Become an Australian Marine Conservation Society Sea Guardian or donate to AMCS. Online at www.amcs.org.au or email: amcs@amcs.org.au or call +61 (7) 3393 5811.

• Join the AMCS Ocean Activists list and sign its online letter to write to the Australian, New South Wales and Queensland Governments to urge for greater protection of grey nurse shark critical habitats. Visit www.amcs.org.au and send your letter today.

FACT BOX

COMMON NAME: Grey nurse shark

SCIENTIFIC NAME: *Carcharias taurus*

STATUS: Critically Endangered (Australian East Coast population: Qld-NSW. Extinct in Victoria).

POPULATION: Fewer than 500 individuals probably remain on the east coast of Australia. Without proper protection it may become extinct in as little as 40 years.

LIFESPAN: Aquaria: 16 years. Wild populations: Unknown, but likely to live longer than aquarium species.

RANGE: Once distributed throughout the world's sub-tropical to cool temperate coastal waters. Now restricted to tropical and temperate waters in the Atlantic, Indian and western Pacific oceans.

THREATS: Incidental and illegal capture by recreational and commercial fishers, illegal shark finning and shark control programmes.

Australian
Marine
Conservation
Society

GURNEY'S PITTA

'ONE OF THE RAREST AND MOST BEAUTIFUL BIRDS OF SOUTH-EAST ASIA, FACING EXTINCTION DUE TO THE WHOLESALE DESTRUCTION OF ITS FOREST HABITAT' BIRDLIFE INTERNATIONAL

The Gurney's pitta is a brilliantly coloured, but secretive bird of the forest floor – also sometimes called the 'Jewel-thrush'. Only known from peninsular Thailand and adjacent southern Myanmar, it has a remarkable history. It was discovered in 1875, fairly widely collected and reported in the 1910s and 1920s, but last seen in 1936. Then, in 1986, a small population was rediscovered in southern Thailand, where around 20 pairs are now known to still exist.

In 2003, the ornithological world was stunned to hear the discovery of a new, much larger population of the pitta in Myanmar. However, large areas of this species' habitat are in danger of being cleared. As a result, in 2005 the British Birdwatching Fair raised £200,000 towards helping to conserve Gurney's pittas in south-east Asia. The bird epitomises many of the problems facing tropical rainforest species. Its greatest threats come from habitat destruction, with forest clearances for palm oil being a particular problem.

FACT BOX

COMMON NAME: Gurney's pitta

SCIENTIFIC NAME: *Pitta gurneyi*

STATUS: Critically endangered

POPULATION: Between 50-100 birds

LIFESPAN: About five years

RANGE: Occurs at one site in peninsular Thailand, and also in adjacent southern Tenasserim, Myanmar.

THREATS: The key reason for its decline has been the almost total clearance of lowland forest in southern Myanmar and peninsular Thailand through clear-felling for timber, unofficial logging and conversion to agriculture. By 1987, only 20-50km^2 of forest below 100m remained in peninsular Thailand, and this area continues to decline. Snare-line trapping for the cage-bird trade is also a serious threat.

WHAT YOU CAN DO...

• Visit the British Birdwatching Fair, held every summer at Britain's Rutland Water. Profits from the fair go towards conservation of species – such as the Gurney's pitta – and habitats around the world.

• Find out more about the work of BirdLife International and its partners by visiting www.birdlife.org.

HAWAIIAN COTTON TREE

'WITH NEW PLANTS AVAILABLE AND CAREFUL CROSSING, THERE IS HOPE FOR RESTORING THIS BEAUTIFUL SPECIES TO THE WILD'
CENTER FOR PLANT CONSERVATION

Native plants are key to maintaining life on Earth. Through pervasive habitat loss and invasive species, however, many native plant species are now imperiled. *Kokia cookei*, also known as the Hawaiian cotton tree, is one of the rarest plant species in the world. It's one of more than 630 imperiled US species with seeds or cuttings secure in the Center for Plant Conservation's National Collection of Endangered Plants, cared for by 34 botanical institutions.

The last known wild plants disappeared in the early 1900s, although a single seed-grown plant survived in cultivation until 1978. After the death of the last whole individual, Waimea Arboretum continued propagating a few clonal plants through grafting, but seeds from these plants usually were weak and short-lived. After many years of work, scientists at Harold L Lyon Arboretum are producing whole plants on their own rootstock, using tissue culture techniques with seed embryos. With new plants available and careful crossing, there is hope for restoring this beautiful species to the wild.

FACT BOX

COMMON NAME: Hawaiian cotton tree

SCIENTIFIC NAME: *Kokia cookei*

STATUS: Extinct in the wild

DESCRIPTION: This 12-15ft-high deciduous tree, closely related to cotton, sports lobed leaves and boasts stunning red undulating flowers.

POPULATION: About 23 plants in cultivation in five different locations.

RANGE: The species occurred in the Hawaiian islands in the dryland forests on Molokai, a habitat mostly destroyed.

THREATS: Exotic, invasive plants, heavy grazing, habitat conversion to agriculture, lack of naturally rooted plants, lack of viable seed production.

WHAT YOU CAN DO...

• Join the Center for Plant Conservation's Friends programme to support work assisting 34 botanic gardens with conservation programmes. Speak to your local or national lawmakers about the need to support plant conservation. Volunteer at your local botanic garden.

• Find out more about CPC's work in Hawaii and the rest of the United States by visiting the Center for Plant Conservation's website at www.centerforplantconservation.org.

Center for
PLANT
Conservation

HEMIPHLEBIA DAMSELFLY

'THEY HAVE SURVIVED THE EXTINCTION OF DINOSAURS AND SEVERAL ICE AGES... BUT CAN DRAGONFLIES SURVIVE THE INCREASING PRESSURES IMPOSED BY MANKIND?' BRITISH DRAGONFLY SOCIETY

Dragonflies are amazing insects with fascinating behaviour and majestic powers of flight. The species around today – such as the endangered Hemiphlebia damselfly – are closely related to the huge insects that flew over the carboniferous forests 300 million years ago, before the dinosaurs roamed the Earth. Dragonflies belong to an order of insects known as the Odonata (meaning toothed jaws), which include the delicate damselflies as well the larger, more powerful 'true' dragonflies.

Changing agricultural practices mean that dragonflies have to face threats such as pollution from fertilisers, insecticides and herbicides; the disappearance of farmland ponds; or the overstocking of ponds with fish – one of the predators of their larvae. The loss of suitable habitats is one of the main threats to dragonfly populations around the world; this can be caused by climate change and increasing droughts, or by growing urban developments and changes in land management.

WHAT YOU CAN DO...

• Dig a pond for dragonflies. Although garden ponds cannot compensate for the loss of natural habitats, they are nonetheless of considerable value for dragonflies. As a gardener, you can also help if you stop buying peat-based compost. This is one practical step towards halting the loss of peat bogs, which are home to many of the rarer species.

• Find out more about the British Dragonfly Society (BDS) by visiting www.dragonflysoc.org.uk or by phoning +44 (0) 1743 282021, and become a BDS member.

FACT BOX

COMMON NAME: Hemiphlebia damselfly

SCIENTIFIC NAME: *Hemiphlebia mirabilis*

STATUS: Endangered worldwide

SIZE: Wingspan = 22mm; body length = 24mm

POPULATION: The exact worldwide population is not known. *Hemiphlebia mirabilis* is just one of over 5,000 species of dragonflies worldwide, several estimated to be endangered or at threat.

LIFESPAN: One year, including over 10 months as an underwater larva and only a few weeks as a colourful flying adult.

RANGE: Restricted to just a few freshwater swamps in Australia.

THREATS: Many of the vegetated flood plain lagoons suitable for the damselfly have been severely altered as a result of land clearing, wetland drainage, river regulation and cattle grazing. Uncontrolled heathland fires also threaten the adults' terrestrial habitats.

BDS
British Dragonfly Society

JAGUAR

'LARGE AREAS OF UNDISTURBED HABITAT MUST BE DESIGNATED AS RESERVES IN ORDER TO PROTECT JAGUARS EFFECTIVELY' RAINFOREST CONCERN

The jaguar is the largest cat on the American continent, and one of the most majestic animals in the world. Like most species of cat, they are solitary animals with large territories: a single male needs between 15sq.km and 45sq.km of undisturbed habitat to survive.

Jaguars inhabit mostly deciduous and tropical rainforest but are also found in habitats ranging from wet savanna to montane areas. However, logging, mining for natural resources and land clearance for farming are destroying rainforests at an alarming rate and fragmenting the primary habitat of this

species. Jaguars are also known to prey on domestic livestock and are therefore targeted by ranchers as pests.

As a result of these threats, they have been virtually eliminated from much of the drier northern parts of its range, as well as through Uruguay and the pampas scrub grasslands of Argentina.

WHAT YOU CAN DO...

● Sponsor an acre of forest (visit the website www.rainforestconcern.org) to protect prime jaguar habitat in South America.

● Avoid buying products with palm oil in them. One in 10 supermarket products contain palm oil, and forest clearance for oil palm plantations is one of the primary threats to the world's rainforests, affecting not only south-east Asia, but increasingly also Latin America.

FACT BOX

COMMON NAME: Jaguar (from the South American Guarani Indian word meaning 'beast that kills with one leap'.

SCIENTIFIC NAME: *Panthera onca*

STATUS: Near Threatened (population declining)

POPULATION: Estimates of total population size range from 15,000-50,000 mature breeding individuals, with a declining trend due to persecution and degradation of its habitat and prey base.

LIFESPAN: Jaguars can live from 15-20 years.

RANGE: Northwards from central Patagonia in South America, occasionally as far north as the southern United States.

THREATS: Man-made habitat loss and fragmentation due to cattle ranching, agriculture, urbanization. Jaguars continue to be hunted illegally.

JAVAN LEAF MONKEY

'THIS ENDEMIC INDONESIAN PRIMATE IS THREATENED BY HUNTING AND POACHING' PROFAUNA INDONESIA

At least 2,500 Javan leaf monkeys are hunted every year, for both the pet trade and the meat trade, particularly at Saradan-Ngawi in East Java. In addition, the species is often sold as a pet on the side of the road, painted by the vendors in garish colours to draw attention to it.

There are several bird markets, too, in which this monkey can be found for sale: Pramuka Bird Market, Bratang Surabaya, Kupang Surabaya, Sukahaji Bandung and Ngasem Jogyakarta being a few examples.

Meanwhile, in Banyuwangi, East Java, the monkey is frequently eaten at parties, where it is prized as an accompaniment to alcohol, and in some quarters even believed to be a cure for asphyxia. And all this despite the fact that the Javan leaf monkey is a protected primate. Often stolen from national parks, the species is in great danger of falling in number to unsustainable levels.

WHAT YOU CAN DO...

● Find out more about ProFauna's Indonesian campaign to stop leaf monkey trade by visiting www.profauna.org

● Visit the same website to discover how you can help ProFauna International save a wide range of threatened Indonesian wildlife.

FACT BOX

COMMON NAME: Javan leaf monkey or Javan langur

LATIN NAME: *Trachypitecus auratuss*

STATUS: Protected by law in Indonesia, CITES Apendix II

POPULATION: Unknown. At least 2,500 are illegally hunted every year

LIFESPAN: Up to 12 years in captivity: its lifespan in the wild has not yet been determined

RANGE: The Indonesian islands of Java, Bali and Lombok

THREATS: Hunting and trading, for both the meat trade and the pet trade. In addition, in Banyuwangi, East Java, the monkey is frequently eaten at parties, where it is prized as an accompaniment to alcohol, and in some quarters believed to be a cure for asphyxia.

ProFauna®
INDONESIA

JOCOTOCO ANTPITTA

'THE TOTAL WORLD POPULATION OF THIS NEWLY DISCOVERED SPECIES IS PROBABLY ONLY A FEW HUNDRED' FUNDACIÓN JOCOTOCO

The Jocotoco antpitta can be considered emblematic of the hundreds of endemic and threatened animals, and thousands of such plant species which are found in the tropical Andes. It was discovered in the cloud forest of the Amazon basin in Ecuador in November 1997, and in January 1998, Fundación Jocotoco (FJ) was established with a mission to protect this amazing bird in its habitat.

The known population is only about 50 birds, of which 75% are now protected inside the foundation's Cerro Tapichalaca reserve. The total world population is probably only about a few hundred, and its habitat is fragmented and depleted by deforestation, burning during dry spells, and cattle farming.

By 2006 FJ had formed eight reserves providing protected habitat for nearly 50 threatened bird species, many large mammals (including spectacled bear, mountain tapir, and jaguar), dozens of threatened Andean frogs, and hundreds of endemic/threatened plants.

WHAT YOU CAN DO...

- By supporting Fundación Jocotoco's programme to protect threatened species in the Andes, either by increasing the size of the reserves, or by helping fund the long-term management of them, by employing local people.

- Visit its website: www.fjocotoco.org.

FACT BOX

COMMON NAME: Jocotoco antpitta ('Jocotoco' is the local name imitating the bird's call)

SCIENTIFIC NAME: *Grallaria ridgelyi*

STATUS: Endangered

POPULATION: Only 50 known individuals; likely estimated world total: a few hundred.

LIFESPAN: Not known – probably about 10 years

RANGE: Very small range, found in a 2300-2700m altitude band (about 1-2km wide) in wet cloud forest along about 50km of Andean east slope in the far south of Ecuador, Rio Chinchipe.

THREATS: Habitat loss and serious fragmentation through forest clearance, burning and cattle farming.

KIPUNJI

'AFRICA'S "NEWEST" MONKEY IS ALSO ONE OF THE WORLD'S RAREST'
SOUTHERN HIGHLANDS CONSERVATION PROGRAMME

First discovered by scientists from the Wildlife Conservation Society's Southern Highlands Conservation Programme as recently as 2004, the kipunji was first thought to be a mangabey. However, genetic and skeletal analysis in 2006 showed the animal to belong to an entirely new genus, the first new genus of African monkey for over 80 years. That such a discovery could be made in East Africa, a region whose wildlife was assumed to be well known, astonished biologists and further demonstrated the considerable biological value of Tanzania's remote and neglected Southern Highlands.

Unsurprisingly Africa's 'newest' monkey is also one of the world's rarest. The kipunji is very seriously threatened from illegal logging and habitat change, especially on Mt Rungwe which holds the largest population. Forest destruction is not only reducing the monkey's habitat but also forcing it out of the forest to raid crops and be hunted in the process.

WHAT YOU CAN DO...

• Support the Kipunji Fund by visiting www.kipunji.org.

• Visit www.southernhighlandstz.org to find out more about the work of the Southern Highlands Conservation Programme on the kipunji and other wildlife.

FACT BOX

COMMON NAME: Kipunji

SCIENTIFIC NAME: *Rungwecebus kipunji*

STATUS: Yet to be classified, but probably critically endangered.

POPULATION: A census is currently on-going, but the total global population is estimated to be fewer than 1,000 individuals.

LIFESPAN: As it is so newly discovered, the kipunji's lifespan is not yet known. The photos shown here are virtually the only ones in existence.

RANGE: The kipunji only occurs in montane forest in southwest Tanzania at altitudes between 1,300-2,450m in about 70km^2 of Rungwe-Livingstone and about 3km^2 of Ndundulu forests.

THREATS: Logging, charcoal-making, poaching and unmanaged resource extraction are common. Widely hunted by humans as retribution for, and prevention against, the raiding of crops.

Southern Highlands Conservation Programme

WILDLIFE CONSERVATION SOCIETY

LEATHERBACK TURTLE

'MARINE TURTLES HAVE SWUM OUR OCEANS FOR AT LEAST 110 MILLION YEARS, BUT IN JUST THE LAST 100 YEARS MANKIND HAS THREATENED THEIR EXISTENCE' MARINE CONSERVATION SOCIETY

Unlike other reptiles, leatherback turtles generate their own body heat and are insulated by a thick layer of fat. This allows them to dive to depths of over 1,000m and migrate thousands of kilometres across the ocean from their tropical nesting beaches to cooler seas in search of their favourite jellyfish prey.

These incredible migrations are hazardous and thousands of leatherbacks entangle and drown in fishing nets set inshore in the tropics, get snagged on swordfish and tuna long-lines set on the high seas, and occasionally get caught in the buoy ropes of crab and lobster pots set in temperate waters. They also eat floating marine litter, such as plastic bags and balloons, probably mistaking them for jellyfish. Once ingested, plastic can block a turtle's gut and lead to death by starvation.

These and other threats mean that without our help the critically endangered leatherback faces an uncertain future.

FACT BOX

COMMON NAME: Leatherback turtle

SCIENTIFIC NAME: *Dermochelys coriacea*

STATUS: Critically endangered

POPULATION: In 1996 scientists estimated that there were between 26,200-42,900 adult female leatherbacks nesting on beaches around the world.

LIFESPAN: Unknown, but like the closely related terrestrial tortoises, the leatherback's life may span many decades.

RANGE: The most widespread reptile on earth and occurs in all ocean basins and the Mediterranean Sea.

THREATS: Climate change, interaction with coastal and high seas fishing gear, egg harvest, nesting beach development, marine litter and over-exploitation for meat.

WHAT YOU CAN DO...

● Turtles can die after swallowing marine litter, so make sure yours doesn't get in the sea. The Marine Conservation Society (MCS) aims to protect our seas, shores and wildlife and campaigns for litter-free seas. To find out more, call MCS on +44 (0) 1989 566017 or visit www.mcsuk.org.

● Adopt-a-Turtle with MCS. Help conservation projects around the world that MCS supports. Contact MCS or visit www.mcsuk.org.

Marine Conservation Society

LITTLE WHIRLPOOL RAM'S-HORN SNAIL

'GLOBAL WARMING PROBABLY POSES THE GREATEST SINGLE THREAT TO THIS AND MANY OTHER RARE SPECIES' CONCHOLOGICAL SOCIETY OF GREAT BRITAIN & IRELAND

*A*nisus vorticulus is a rare and vulnerable mollusc, confined to an equally scarce and endangered habitat, that of flood plain and coastal grazing marsh. These are typically flat expanses adjacent to the slow-flowing lower reaches of rivers where farmers have traditionally grazed animals and cut meadows for hay. Grazing marshes are typically bisected by networks of freshwater drains, and this species lives in the clean waters of only a few of the most pristine channels, always in association with a rich diversity of other freshwater animals and plants.

This snail is at risk from many factors. The conversion of traditionally managed areas to arable crops and intensive grass production typically lowers ditch water levels and adds fertiliser run-off. This 'junk-food' for plants creates 'over-enriched' waters that kill the snail together with other freshwater plants and animals. A final and increasing danger is global warming. Sea-level rise threatens all *Anisus* sites with saltwater intrusion.

WHAT YOU CAN DO...

• Support sustainable national, local and personal lifestyle policies that minimise greenhouse emissions. Global warming probably poses the greatest single threat to this snail and many other rare species that are living in habitats only found in lowland areas close to sea level.

• Find out more about the conservation work of the Conchological Society of Great Britain & Ireland by visiting www.conchsoc.org.

FACT BOX

COMMON NAME: Little whirlpool ram's-horn snail

SCIENTIFIC NAME: *Anisus vorticulus*

STATUS: UK BAP Priority species, and also appears on two European Union 'Habitats Directive' annexes, II and IV

POPULATION: In the UK only known from a few ditches in the Norfolk Broads, Pevensey Levels and Arun Valley in West Sussex, where it is declining. Populations have been lost from Lewes in Sussex and Staines in Surrey within the last 30 years.

LIFESPAN: The snail has an annual life cycle.

RANGE: Occurs very locally throughout central and southern Europe.

THREATS: Agricultural fertilisers and changes of land use from traditional grazing to intensive agricultural practices; removal of grazing cattle; over-frequent dredging. An increasing threat is from sea-level rise leading to the saltwater flooding of ditches.

LONESOME GEORGE

'LONESOME GEORGE IS A DAILY REMINDER OF HOW MUCH THERE IS TO DO TO MAKE SURE OTHER SPECIES DON'T GO DOWN THE SAME PATH' CHARLES DARWIN FOUNDATION

The loneliest animal on the planet and a tragic story of human impact on a unique ecosystem is that of 'Lonesome George', the last known survivor of the Pinta Island species of the Galapagos giant tortoise.

Giant tortoises once roamed the Galapagos archipelago in their hundreds of thousands. Whalers and sealers heavily depleted their numbers in the nineteenth century for food. With tortoises thought to be already gone from Pinta Island, goats were released by fishermen in the 1950s as an alternative food source. These destroyed the vegetation and directly competed with any remaining tortoises for food. In 1971, a single male tortoise was found, who now lives at the Charles Darwin Foundation's research station in Galapagos. A worldwide search has failed to find Lonesome George a mate, and thorough searches of Pinta Island have found no evidence of other living tortoises. For possibly a century to come he will stand as a living reminder of what has been lost on our planet.

FACT BOX

COMMON NAME: Pinta Island Galapagos giant tortoise, aka 'Lonesome George'

SCIENTIFIC NAME: *Geochelone abingdoni*

STATUS: Extinct in the wild

SIZE: May weigh up to 250kg and measure 150cm over the curve of the carapace.

POPULATION: One surviving individual.

LIFESPAN: Approximately 100-200 years.

RANGE: Pinta Island, located in the North of the Galapagos archipelago.

THREATS: Habitat destruction by introduced goats, predation by man.

fundacion
Charles Darwin
foundation

WHAT YOU CAN DO...

● Your commitment and support will help secure a sustainable future for the Galapagos ecosystem. Help protect its unique species (visit the website www.darwinfoundation.org or email: cdrs@fcdarwin.org.ec).

● CDF works with a wide network of partners. To directly support these efforts visit www.darwinfoundation.org/en/get-involved/fogo to see how you can help.

LONG-EARED OWL

'GREATER AWARENESS OF THIS OWL IS NEEDED TO ENSURE ITS CONSERVATION' HAWK AND OWL TRUST

If there was a prize for the least-known bird in Britain, the long-eared owl would be the winner. This secretive, nocturnal bird with its cryptic plumage is extraordinarily good at hiding and even its call is soft and easily missed.

Competition with its arch-rival the tawny owl could be one of the limiting factors. It is the commonest owl in Ireland where there are no tawnies.

The long-eared owl is a bird of the forest edge and small copses, and in some places it even nests in small hawthorns in hedgerows. Massive hedge removal in the second half of the twentieth century and loss of lowland heathland – one of its favoured hunting grounds – to housing and other developments have diminished the population.

Artificial wicker baskets, if there is a scarcity of natural nest sites, have been successful where there are suitable feeding areas. Greater awareness of this owl is needed to ensure its conservation.

FACT BOX

COMMON NAME: Long-eared owl

SCIENTIFIC NAME: *Asio otus*

STATUS: Protected under the EU Birds Directive

POPULATION: Some 1,100 to 3,600 breeding pairs in England, Scotland and Wales, with a similar number in Ireland. European status 205,000 (2% in Britain and Ireland).

LIFESPAN: 52% mortality in first year; oldest wild owl is a long-eared at more than 27 years.

RANGE: Resident in much of Europe, northern Asia and North America.

THREATS: Loss of habitat and lack of knowledge as often overlooked.

WHAT YOU CAN DO...

• Take part in the Hawk and Owl Trust's ongoing survey on long-eared owls each March (visit www.hawkandowl.org, or contact Hawk and Owl Trust, PO Box 100, Taunton TA4 2WX, Tel: +44 (0) 870 990 3889).

• Adopt a Box (website as above). The money raised helps the Trust with its conservation projects including long-eared owls.

Hawk
and
Owl
Trust

MANGROVE FINCH

'"DARWIN'S" FINCHES, ONCE A CATALYST FOR EVOLUTIONARY THINKING, ARE NOW AN INDICATOR OF HOW THINGS CAN GO WRONG WHEN MAN INTRUDES UPON NATURE' GALAPAGOS CONSERVANCY

No animal has had a more profound impact on the way we see the world than the finches of Galapagos. The finches, through adaptive radiation, are the foremost example of evolution at work. The most endangered of 'Darwin's' finches, the mangrove finch inhabits the naturally scarce mangrove forests of the western Galapagos Islands, which in recent years have become vulnerable to destruction.

Further threatened by introduced animals, the mangrove finch is one of the rarest birds on the planet. For more than a decade, the Charles Darwin Foundation (CDF) has carried out research aimed to halt the decline of the finch and restore its habitat, safeguarding the unique niche occupied by this bird. Restoration projects have had a history of success and doing the impossible in these amazing islands. The CDF, through exacting science supporting excellent management, aims to ensure that the mangrove finch does not become another sad addition to the extinct species of our planet.

FACT BOX

COMMON NAME: Mangrove finch

SCIENTIFIC NAME: *Cactospiza heliobates*

STATUS: Endangered

POPULATION: Estimated to be no more than 40-50 pairs

LIFESPAN: Approx five to 10 years

RANGE: Restricted to the mangrove swamps or forests of southern Isabela Island, which have been considerably reduced by man.

THREATS: Habitat destruction, introduced species such as cats, black rats, anis, fire ants and the fly *Philornis*.

GALAPAGOS
C O N S E R V A N C Y
Saving one of the world's great treasures

MARINE IGUANA

'AS SOON AS THEIR EGGS ARE LAID, THESE CREATURES ARE UNDER THREAT FROM SPECIES INTRODUCED TO THE ISLANDS BY THE HUMAN RACE' GALAPAGOS CONSERVATION TRUST

The first time you see a marine iguana underwater it makes you realise just how new to the earth human beings are. Marine iguanas resemble ancient dinosaurs of the ocean and have populated the earth for millions of years. Let's not allow the presence of humans wipe these fascinating creatures out forever.

The Galapagos marine iguana is the world's only sea-going lizard, and it is found on all of the main islands of the Galapagos.

There are seven subspecies which vary considerably in size and colour from island to island. The ones on Espanola are the most brightly coloured and sometimes called the 'Christmas Tree' marine iguana.

Marine iguanas live mainly on land, where they warm up in the sun, since they are cold blooded. Although most marine iguanas feed on algae in the intertidal zones, the largest animals on each island can dive up to 20m deep.

FACT BOX

COMMON NAME: Marine iguana

SCIENTIFIC NAME: *Amblyrhynchus cristatus*

STATUS: Vulnerable

POPULATION: Fluctuates between 37,000 and 280,000

LIFESPAN: Around 30 years

RANGE: Restricted to the intertidal zones and islands surrounding the Galapagos archipelago.

THREATS: Predation from introduced species such as rats, cats and dogs is a large factor contributing to the marine iguana's demise. Populations can severely drop during *El Nino* (a large-scale climatic fluctuation of the tropical Pacific Ocean), due to a lack of food supply. The marine iguana is a vulnerable species due to its island endemicity.

Galapagos Conservation Trust

MARSH FRITILLARY

'BUTTERFLIES ARE AMONG THE MOST BEAUTIFUL AND FASCINATING CREATURES ON THE PLANET, BUT THEIR NUMBERS ARE DWINDLING RAPIDLY AS BREEDING HABITATS ARE DESTROYED'
BUTTERFLY CONSERVATION

Butterflies represent both the beauty and fragility of nature, but it's a sad fact that they are declining faster than most other groups of wildlife. They are very sensitive to change and are valuable indicators of the health of the environment: where butterflies thrive, nature is in balance.

The marsh fritillary epitomises the threats facing butterflies. Its caterpillars feed on just one main food-plant, Devil's-bit Scabious, which grows in unfertilised, flower-rich pastures. Suitable habitats are maintained by low intensity, traditional grazing, usually by cattle.

However, such habitats have been lost at a staggering rate across Europe as pastures are converted to arable land, drained, or 'improved' with artificial fertiliser. In the UK, over 92% of such pastures were lost during the twentieth century, leaving remaining patches small and isolated.

FACT BOX

COMMON NAME: Marsh fritillary

SCIENTIFIC NAME: *Euphydryas aurinia*

STATUS: Vulnerable, owing to rapid decline across Europe.

POPULATION: Exact European population not known but around 400 colonies are estimated to survive in the UK. Populations are renowned for their large fluctuations, which make them especially prone to local extinction. They therefore need extensive areas of breeding habitat to survive.

LIFESPAN: A single generation per year, with adults living just five to 10 days.

RANGE: Found across Europe.

THREATS: Continued habitat destruction and lack of suitable management. Habitat fragmentation is a growing threat.

WHAT YOU CAN DO...

• Join Butterfly Conservation and support its work to save butterflies and moths in the UK and across Europe. You can also contribute to its world-beating recording and monitoring schemes.

• Find out more about its work and join online at www.butterfly-conservation.org or phone +44 (0) 870 7744 309.

Butterfly Conservation
Saving butterflies, moths and their habitats

MEDITERRANEAN MONK SEAL

'THIS IS ONE OF THE RAREST MAMMALS IN THE WORLD, AND THE MOST ENDANGERED MARINE MAMMAL IN EUROPE' EURONATUR

Mediterranean monk seals were once widespread all over the Mediterranean, the Black Sea and the adjacent Atlantic coast. Nowadays only 400-500 individuals remain, dispersed into small groups. Having been hunted for centuries, monk seals have left the beaches and withdrawn into caves and inaccessible creeks. Yet expanding tourist activities intrude on the habitats of these shy animals even in those hidden caves where they rear their pups. The over-exploitation of fish by industrial fishing has caused a shortage of the monk seal's food. Additionally, monk seals continue to be hunted by fishermen since they prey on fish caught in nets, in which they may get entangled and drown.

In order to save this species, there is an urgent need to establish, maintain and guard protected areas in which animals can raise their young undisturbed. Other important measures are environmental education and support for coastal fishermen in finding alternative income and fishing methods.

WHAT YOU CAN DO...

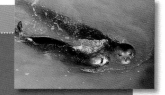

● Support one of the local projects coordinated in conjunction with Euronatur (www.euronatur.org) in order to protect the remaining Mediterranean monk seal populations and improve the situation of this critically endangered species.

● Get informed about the threats to marine mammals and how you can help by visiting OceanCare at www.oceancare.org. With your support it can continue to apply its experience in protection of marine mammals and the oceans.

FACT BOX

COMMON NAME: Mediterranean monk seal

LATIN NAME: *Monachus monachus*

STATUS: Critically endangered

POPULATION: By 2004 the population was estimated to range between 400-500 individuals, split up into several small groups. At present, the largest populations live at the Atlantic coast of Mauritania, in Madeira, in the archipelagos of the Greek and Turkish Aegean and in southern Turkey.

LIFESPAN: Mediterranean monk seals can live up to 30 years or more.

RANGE: Today's population is restricted to a few places in the eastern and southern Mediterranean and the Atlantic.

THREATS: Loss of habitat, overfishing, entanglement in fishing nets and direct persecution by fishermen, disturbance at breeding places, chemical pollution.

ocean care
www.oceancare.org

EURONATUR

MILKY STORK

'IN MALAYSIA, THE MILKY STORK HAS DECLINED TO JUST A FEW BIRDS AND IS CERTAIN TO BECOME EXTINCT IN THE NEAR FUTURE'
WETLANDS INTERNATIONAL

The milky stork is a large waterbird with limited presence in south-east Asia, primarily associated with coastal mangroves. In the last 20 years, this handsome species has suffered from habitat loss, human disturbance and hunting activities across its range.

In Malaysia, it has declined from over 100 individual birds in the 1980s to just a few remaining birds and is certain to become extinct in the near future. The population in Cambodia is also very small. In Indonesia, mainly Sumatra and Java, far fewer birds have been observed in recent times, compared to an estimated 5,000-6,000 birds in the 1980s.

Wetlands International monitors, with its partners, the remaining populations and works on the recovery of mangrove areas. Further study on its status, protection of its remaining habitats, reduction of human disturbance and persecution, increased awareness and a re-introduction programme in Malaysia, are key for its survival.

FACT BOX

COMMON NAME: Milky stork

SCIENTIFIC NAME: *Mycteria cinerea*

STATUS: Vulnerable

POPULATION: Fewer than 5,000 individuals

LIFESPAN: Twenty years

RANGE: Limited in south-east Asia. Mainly found in Indonesia, with very small numbers seen in Malaysia and Cambodia.

THREATS: Habitat loss, human disturbance and hunting are the major threats to the survival of the species.

WHAT YOU CAN DO...

● Support Wetlands International's field study and habitat conservation efforts – for more information visit www.wetlands.org. You can also support bird monitoring work in your country. To find out more, email: simon.delany@wetlands.org.

● Get informed about this bird and support the work of Wetlands International by purchasing the booklet 'Status Overview and Recommendations for the Conservation of Milky Stork in Malaysia', for US$10 minimum by emailing: malaysia@wetlands.org.my.

WETLANDS INTERNATIONAL

MONARCH BUTTERFLY

'MIGRATORY MONARCH POPULATIONS FACE MULTIPLE THREATS, INCLUDING ILLEGAL LOGGING AND CLIMATE CHANGE'
THE ENTOMOLOGICAL FOUNDATION

Flying over 2,000 miles to a tiny fir grove high in the mountains of central Mexico that it has never seen, the monarch butterfly makes one of the most remarkable migrations on earth. Orange and black monarchs are among the most recognizable insects throughout the Americas, and their strong flight has carried them to Australia and other Pacific nations. But only in North America do monarchs perform long-distance migrations. The monarchs that migrate from the northernmost latitudes in the fall don't make it back in the spring – but their grandchildren do.

Migratory monarch populations face multiple threats. The Mexican fir groves they rely on for winter survival are increasingly isolated, threatened by illegal logging, and possibly climate change. Efficient agricultural weed control and changing land use patterns in much of their breeding range are reducing populations of the milkweeds that are the only food of monarch caterpillars.

FACT BOX

COMMON NAME: Monarch butterfly

SCIENTIFIC NAME: *Danaus plexippus*

STATUS: Currently stable, but potentially vulnerable.

POPULATION: Wintering migratory population perhaps 50-100 million. In some years, possibly up to 200 million.

LIFESPAN: Overwintering populations, up to nine months. Summer generations two to three months (including larval and pupal stages).

RANGE: North and South America, Australia, many Pacific Islands. Migratory populations restricted to North America.

THREATS: Greatest threat is habitat destruction or modification in Mexican wintering groves; agricultural weed management also reduces availability of larval host plants.

The Entomological Foundation
Exciting Youth about Science through Insects

WHAT YOU CAN DO...

• If you live in the relevant areas, plant native milkweeds in your garden to provide host plants for monarch caterpillars.

• Support The Entomological Foundation and Monarch Watch. Visit www.entfdn.org for details.

MULGARA

'MULGARAS ARE DECLINING THROUGHOUT THEIR RANGE AS THE DESERT DUNES ARE INCREASINGLY BEING USED FOR CATTLE GRAZING'
AUSTRALIAN BUSH HERITAGE FUND

The bright eyes of the mulgara are not seen very often in the Australian desert. This elusive small marsupial is usually down a burrow by day, away from the scorching sun, and only emerges at night to hunt or find a mate. The females carry and suckle their young in a pouch.

The size of individual populations varies depending on rainfall. Good rains in the desert produce a flush of vegetation. Insects and small rodents thrive at these times and provide abundant food for the mulgaras and their numbers increase. As the desert dries up again, food availability declines and population numbers fall.

Aside from normal population fluctuations that result from the weather, mulgaras are declining throughout their range as the desert dunes are increasingly being used for cattle grazing. With the cattle and people come the predators, and with domestication of the land comes the increasing risk of broad-acre wildfires that destroy habitat.

WHAT YOU CAN DO...

• You can help protect this species by donating to the Australian Bush Heritage Fund. This organisation has already purchased two properties in the Outback to help protect the mulgara and other desert animals. It needs your support to manage the land to ensure these species survive, and also buy more land. Visit www.bushheritage.org +61 (3) 8610 9100

• You can volunteer on the Bush Heritage preserves, helping to care for the land, and perhaps assist with research conducted on small desert animals by the Institute of Wildlife Research, University of Sydney. Visit www.bushheritage.org.

FACT BOX

COMMON NAME: Mulgara

SCIENTIFIC NAME: *Dasycercus cristicauda*

STATUS: Nationally vulnerable

SIZE: The Mulgara is about 180mm (7in) from nose to tip of tail with a total body weight between 70-170g (2–5 oz)

POPULATION: Mulgaras were once widespread and common throughout the central desert region of Australia. Now the population is declining and fragmented into small, discontinuous populations.

LIFESPAN: At least three years.

RANGE: The mulgara lives in the arid dunes of the deserts of Queensland, the Northern Territory and Western Australia.

THREATS: Grazing and trampling of the sheltering vegetation by domestic stock, uncontrolled wildfires and predation by introduced predators such as red foxes and feral cats are the greatest threats to the survival of this species.

AUSTRALIAN BUSH HERITAGE FUND

NATTERJACK TOAD

'LOCAL EXTINCTIONS HAVE RESULTED IN THE DISAPPEARANCE OF THIS SPECIALIST AMPHIBIAN FROM MORE THAN 75% OF ITS FORMER HAUNTS'
THE HERPETOLOGICAL CONSERVATION TRUST

Natterjack toads live in some of the most exciting and interesting habitats in Britain – sand dunes, heathland and even the upper reaches of saltmarshes. With short hind legs, they are adapted to hunting their invertebrate prey in places that have plenty of bare ground and very short vegetation. Being good burrowers, they simply dig down into the ground to avoid extremes of temperature and dryness. For breeding they require shallow ephemeral ponds that warm up quickly to speed the tadpoles' development.

Sadly, local extinctions have resulted in the disappearance of this specialist amphibian from more than 75% of its former haunts. Fortunately the female natterjack lays thousands of eggs, and colonies have a great capacity to recover once key habitat features have been restored. The management work might be as straightforward as recreating breeding ponds or increasing the number of stock grazing the site, but this initial work and the ongoing maintenance requires funding.

FACT BOX

COMMON NAME: Natterjack toad

SCIENTIFIC NAME: *Bufo calamita*

STATUS: Vulnerable at the edges of its range, but locally abundant and not endangered in the core.

POPULATION: In Britain there is a total of about 50 colonies.

LIFESPAN: In the wild males can live to about eight or nine years, and females, because of their lower risk of predation, can live to 12-15 years.

RANGE: The world range of this species is western Europe from Spain and Portugal through central northern Europe to the Baltic States of the former USSR, Britain and Sweden.

THREATS: At sites where the habitat has not been used for housing, agriculture or forestry, the main threats are the loss of ephemeral ponds and changes in the terrestrial habitat to favour common anurans.

THE HERPETOLOGICAL CONSERVATION TRUST

WHAT YOU CAN DO...

● Find out more about the work of The Herpetological Conservation Trust and, if you live in Britain, whether natterjacks are found in your part the country. For more information visit www.herpconstruct.org.uk.

● Take part in an organised walk to see and hear natterjack toads in the spring; take part in a habitat management task at a natterjack toad site; offer to help monitor a site near you; help fund the creation of a natterjack toad pond.

NORTHERN RIGHT WHALE

'SADLY, IT WAS BEING THE "RIGHT" WHALE TO HUNT THAT HAS DRIVEN THESE ANIMALS TO NEAR EXTINCTION' WDCS

The northern right whale is the most endangered of the great whales, with their worldwide population is estimated at just a few hundred individuals. Right whales got their name because whalers considered them to be the 'right' whale to hunt as they are easy to approach and catch, float when dead and have a lot of oil in their blubber, known as 'liquid oil', which was sold for many things, including making soap and paint.

Sadly, it was being the 'right' whale to hunt that has driven these animals to near extinction. They live only in the northern hemisphere and today are threatened by habitat loss, human disturbance, entanglement in fishing nets and collisions with ships.

The future of this species is under such threat that the loss of a single right whale each year may lead to the extinction of this species. WDCS is helping to save this species by working to reduce deaths in fishing nets, and campaigning for regulations to reduce ship strikes. Although it is no longer a target for hunters, other species are. WDCS also campaigns to end the needless and inhumane killing of all whales in commercial hunts.

WHAT YOU CAN DO...

- Become a supporter of WDCS, the Whale and Dolphin Conservation Society, and help species like the northern right whale. Visit www.wdcs.org for further information.
  - You can support WDCS by adopting a whale or dolphin, by becoming a member or by signing up to a campaign. For more details on the work of WDCS and how you can help, log on to www.wdcs.org, email info@wdcs.org or call +44 (0) 1249 449 500.

FACT BOX

COMMON NAME: Northern right whale

SCIENTIFIC NAME: *Eubalaena glacialis*

STATUS: Endangered

SIZE: These animals weigh around 1 tonne at birth, and grow to between 30-80 tonnes. An adult whale is usually between 11-18m long.

POPULATION: It is estimated that there are only about 300 individual northern right whales in existence.

RANGE: Northern right whales only live in the northern hemisphere, and the vast majority of them are found in the western North Atlantic, off the coasts of Canada and North America. Only a few individuals are thought to remain in the eastern North Atlantic.

THREATS: Entanglement in fishing gear, vessel strikes, habitat loss, human disturbance and pollution.

WDCS
Whale and Dolphin Conservation Society

ORANGUTAN

'WE ARE ON THE BRINK OF SEEING ONE OF OUR CLOSEST RELATIVES, THE ORANGUTAN, BECOME NEEDLESSLY EXTINCT'
ORANGUTAN FOUNDATION

About a million years ago, orangutans lived throughout much of Asia. Today, their range is much reduced and they are only found in the rapidly disappearing rainforests of Borneo and Sumatra.

Tragically, orangutans have drastically reduced in numbers, particularly over the last decade. This is entirely due to the destruction of their habitat by either logging or the cutting down of rainforest for development of palm oil plantations. Many experts believe that of all the great apes, the orangutan risks being the first to become extinct in the wild unless immediate action is taken to halt these two major threats.

The close relationship between the orangutan and its rainforest home is a highly complex and interdependent one. Much is still to be learnt about this gentle ape, but we do know that if we lose the orangutan we also risk losing the invaluable rainforests as well as one of our closest living relatives.

WHAT YOU CAN DO...

● Join and find out more about the work of the Orangutan Foundation, by visiting www.orangutan.org.uk or by emailing info@orangutan.org.uk.

● Adopt an orangutan (www.orangutan.org.uk). The money raised will go towards helping the Orangutan Foundation protect the species and their rainforest home.

FACT BOX

COMMON NAME: Bornean orangutan and Sumatran orangutan

SCIENTIFIC NAME: *Pongo pygmaeus* and *Pongo abelii*

STATUS: Endangered (Bornean orangutan); Critically endangered (Sumatran orangutan)

POPULATION: Between 50,000-60,000

LIFESPAN: Up to 45 years

RANGE: Borneo and northern Sumatra

THREATS: The rapid spread of palm oil plantations encroaching upon tropical rainforests. Illegal and poorly managed logging within the same forests.

PHILIPPINE EAGLE OWL

'AS BY FAR THE LARGEST OWL IN THE PHILIPPINES, THE OWL IS AT THE TOP OF THE FOOD PYRAMID, AND AS SUCH IS EXTREMELY VULNERABLE TO THE LOSS OF ITS HABITAT' WORLD OWL TRUST

The Philippines has more threatened owls than any other country in the world, due to the destruction of virtually all the lowland rainforest which once covered 75% of the low-lying areas of the country – the home of most Philippine owls and many other species of flora and fauna. The owl is at the top of the food pyramid, and as such is extremely vulnerable to the loss of its habitat – lowland forest near watercourses. Always uncommon, this owl has been recorded from six islands in the past, but the few recent records have all been made in the Sierra Madre mountains of Luzon and only number three to four individuals at three sites.

The World Owl Trust has entered into a Memorandum of Agreement with the Philippine Government to set up and manage the Philippine Owl Conservation Programme – the first ever international owl conservation programme aimed at saving not only endangered Philippine owls, but also the country's overall biodiversity.

FACT BOX

COMMON NAME: Philippine eagle owl

SCIENTIFIC NAME: *Bubo philippensis*

STATUS: Endangered

POPULATION: Unknown, but certainly declining rapidly

LIFESPAN: Unknown. Probably around 25 years.

RANGE: Formerly recorded from six (possibly seven) Philippine islands, but recent records only from northern Luzon.

THREATS: Severe deforestation of lowland tropical rainforests throughout the Philippines, plus probable persecution.

WHAT YOU CAN DO...

● Join the World Owl Trust to give them a louder voice when dealing with the world's governments. World Owl Trust, Muncaster Castle, Ravenglass, Cumbria, CA18 1RQ, England; +44 (0) 1229 717393; www.owls.org.

● Make donations to provide the Trust with the funds to enable them to carry out a survey to determine the current distribution and status of this owl, plus studies of its biology – virtually nothing is currently known about its behaviour, food, nest-site, calls or breeding biology.

PIPING PLOVER

'THE PERMANENT PROTECTION OF KEY SHORELINE BREEDING AREAS IS CRITICAL TO THE SURVIVAL OF THE PIPING PLOVER'
NATURE CONSERVANCY CANADA

Soon after birth, downy piping plover chicks are able to follow their parents looking for insects and worms in the sand, but their chances of survival are slim. These endangered shorebirds lay their eggs on the ground, often on the same beaches frequented by humans. The eggs and young are so well camouflaged that they are often not noticed until they have been trampled or crushed by off-road vehicles.

The eggs are further threatened by changes in water levels due to building activities, dams, and storms. The fledglings, unable to fly for their first 30 days, are appetizing to cats and dogs, and other predators such as gulls and raccoons, attracted by picnickers' litter.

With only 6,000 adult piping plovers remaining worldwide, the permanent protection of key shoreline breeding areas is now critical to the survival of this tiny bird.

FACT BOX

COMMON NAME: Piping plover

SCIENTIFIC NAME: *Charadrius melodus*

STATUS: Endangered in US and Canada

POPULATION: The worldwide population is estimated at 6,000 adults. The Canadian Atlantic populations of the melodus subspecies consists of just 500 adults.

LIFESPAN: Only 13% of females and 28% of males live five years. Maximum age is 11.

RANGE: Piping plovers breed in the Great Plains, on the North American Atlantic Coast, in the Great Lakes and in St Pierre et Miquelon. Wintering grounds from North Carolina to Florida, in the Gulf States, Mexico, and the Caribbean.

THREATS: Destruction and degradation of habitat, human use of beaches, predation, shoreline erosion, nest destruction, and changes in water levels.

WHAT YOU CAN DO...

● Protect critical remaining piping plover habitat on the Great Plains and Atlantic Coast by contributing to the Nature Conservancy of Canada (NCC) at www.natureconservancy.ca. NCC works to protect piping plover habitat by acquiring and permanently protecting the beaches they use for breeding.

● Obey signs posted to protect piping plovers and do not approach their nests. Be careful to properly dispose of all litter when outdoors. When on beaches used by piping plovers, keep your pets on a lead.

NATURE CONSERVANCY
C A N A D A

POLAR BEAR

'DISAPPEARING ICE FLOES ROB POLAR BEARS OF THEIR HUNTING GROUNDS, LEAVING THEM TOO THIN TO REPRODUCE' **NATURE CANADA**

Polar bears are the world's largest land predators, and the most majestic creatures of the Far North. But dramatic changes taking place in the Arctic threaten the survival of this spectacular species.

Global warming is melting the polar ice caps, robbing the bears of the ice floes they need to hunt prey. As the annual sea-ice melts, polar bears are forced ashore to spend their summers fasting. If the Arctic ice cap continues to melt sooner and form later, polar bears will become too thin to reproduce and they'll be extinct by the end of this century.

Increased human activity in the North brings other threats to the polar bear. Because they are at the top of the food chain, polar bears are highly exposed to toxic chemicals ingested by animals they eat.

As shipping traffic increases in the North, spilled oil strips the bear's fur of its insulating properties, and renders the bear's prey inedible.

WHAT YOU CAN DO...

● Support Nature Canada's efforts to save the polar bear's habitat by making a donation at www. naturecanada.ca. Nature Canada is working to protect Canada's Far North from industrialisation and the effects of global warming.

● Climate change affects humans and bears alike. Do your part to slow global warming. Visit www.naturecanada.ca to find out how.

naturecanada.ca

PONDS

'THERE ARE ONLY ABOUT 400,000 PONDS LEFT IN GREAT BRITAIN, COMPARED WITH 1.2M IN 1880' **POND CONSERVATION**

Ponds are beautiful habitats, and great for teaching children about biodiversity. In the UK they are home to about 2,500 animal and 1,000 plant species, many rare and threatened.

In prehistoric times there could have been millions of natural ponds, but the Romans started the process of draining land for agriculture, so most ponds today are man-made. Probably their biggest threat today is pollution from farms and vehicles, causing ecological change. Ponds in ordinary countryside now have half the plant species they should, and they are also threatened by invasive exotic weeds.

It's cheap and easy to create good new ponds if the water quality is right. One new pond complex in Oxfordshire contained a quarter of the UK freshwater fauna and flora after only five years. With climate change coming, it's vital to create more good ponds, so they can be stepping-stones to help species adapt their ranges.

WHAT YOU CAN DO...

● Put in a pond in your garden, or even better, get together with friends to create a new pond in your community, or protect an existing one. Pond Conservation can give advice.

● Find out more by contacting Pond Conservation by visiting www.pondconservation.org.uk, or by emailing info@ pondconservation.org.uk.

FACT BOX

COMMON NAME: Ponds are often also called pools, tarns or lochans.

STATUS: Ponds have declined greatly in numbers and quality during the twentieth century

SIZE: Ponds are still water bodies less than two hectares in area. They can be permanent, or dry out in the summer.

POPULATION: There are only about 400,000 ponds left in Great Britain, compared with 1.2 million in 1880. This decline is probably true for most industrialised countries.

LIFESPAN: Most ponds today are less than 200 years old, although a few date from the ice age about 10,000 years ago. It's natural for new ponds to gradually fill with vegetation, and they are valuable for wildlife in all their stages.

THREATS: Pollution, especially fertilising nutrients that ruin their ecological balance, over-stocking as fishing ponds, and being filled in by farmers or builders.

Pond Conservation
For Life in Fresh Waters

POWELLIPHANTA 'AUGUSTUS'

'THIS SPECIES IS LIKELY TO BECOME EXTINCT BEFORE IT HAS EVEN BEEN FORMALLY NAMED' ECO

The *Powelliphanta* land snails of Aotearoa/New Zealand are of ancient lineage – they were already on board when New Zealand drifted north from the massive continent of Gondwana 84 million years ago. Then, like the moa and weta, the carnivorous *Powelliphanta* land snails developed gigantism, and became jewels in the strange New Zealand world where large flightless invertebrates took the niche occupied elsewhere by small mammals.

One species, *Powelliphanta* 'Augustus', is likely to become extinct before it has even been formally named. This species clings tenuously to its mountain-top existence, as it is overtaken by a coal mine that has already destroyed most of its population and habitat. In April 2006, the New Zealand government gave state-owned coal-mining producer Solid Energy permission to mine 94% of the snails' tiny remaining habitat. A decision that will almost certainly lead to the first state-sponsored species extinction New Zealand has seen.

FACT BOX

COMMON NAME: Augustus snail, native land snail

SCIENTIFIC NAME: *Powelliphanta* 'Augustus'

STATUS: Nationally critical

POPULATION: Around 500

LIFESPAN: Between 12-20 years

RANGE: Five hectares on Mt Augustus, near Westport, South Island, New Zealand.

THREATS: Sadly, 94% of their remaining habitat is to be mined for coal, while the remaining 6% will be subject to rockfall and blast debris. The best scientific evidence, from the Department of Conservation, suggests that this will lead to their extinction, as attempts to move the snails and breed them in captivity seem extremely unlikely to succeed.

WHAT YOU CAN DO...

● Write to Helen Clark, Prime Minister of New Zealand, Parliament Buildings, New Zealand by emailing pm@ministers.govt.nz, and asking why her government has condemned an absolutely protected species to extinction.

● Check out more about Environment and Conservation Organisations (ECO) of Aotearoa/New Zealand by visiting www.eco.org.nz.

PYGMY HOG

'THE WORLD'S SMALLEST PIG IS NOW ONLY FOUND IN ASSAM WHERE A POPULATION OF AROUND 500 ANIMALS MAY EXIST'
DURRELL WILDLIFE CONSERVATION TRUST

The pygmy hog is the world's smallest pig, with adults only reaching a weight of less than 10kg. They once occurred in tall grasslands from Nepal, Bhutan to Assam in north-east India. However, they are now only known to be found in the Manas Tiger Reserve in Assam where a population of around 500 animals may exist.

Habitat loss through uncontrolled burning of the tall grasslands is thought to have been the cause for the species' disappearance throughout most of its former range. These diminutive pigs rely on the thatch for cover from predators, food and uniquely, for the building of their nests for breeding.

Durrell has established a very successful captive breeding programme and plans to release pygmy hogs into protected areas in which they once occurred. Animals will be radio-tracked and monitored to learn more about their home ranges and use of habitat. Durrell also works in conjunction with the Assamese and Indian Forestry Departments in securing the future for this species and other biodiversity of the region.

FACT BOX

COMMON NAME: Pygmy hog

SCIENTIFIC NAME: *Sus salvanius*

STATUS: Critically endangered

LIFESPAN: More than 10 years.

POPULATION: Unknown, but presumed to be less than 500 animals in the wild.

RANGE: Now only known to be found in the Manas Tiger Reserve in Assam.

THREATS: Habitat destruction through uncontrolled burning of the tall grasslands which they rely on for cover from predators, food and for building their nests.

WHAT YOU CAN DO...

• Help fund the conservation of the pygmy hog by becoming a member of Durrell Wildlife Conservation Trust. Join online at www.durrellwildlife.org, telephone +44 (0) 1534 860000 or write for a membership application form to: Durrell Wildlife Conservation Trust, Les Augres Manor, Trinity JE3 5BP.

• Durrell Wildlife Conservation Trust is the only UK charity working to save the pygmy hog. You can help by making a donation to this project or you can leave a legacy to the Trust to help with this, and the Trust's other projects to save endangered species from extinction.

durrell

RAINFOREST

'THE EARTH'S SINGLE GREATEST BIOLOGICAL TREASURE BANK: START SAVING NOW...' WORLD LAND TRUST

Tropical forests have evolved over millions of years to become the store of living and breathing renewable natural resources that they are today. Scientists estimate that more than half of all the world's plant and animal species live in tropical forests.

Not only are they important hotspots for biodiversity, they also perform all kinds of practical services that benefit modern humans. They produce roughly 40% of the Earth's oxygen, essential to life, and suck up air pollution. Climate change is perhaps the biggest environmental threat facing the planet and saving tropical forests will lock up valuable carbon and help off-set the damage caused by modern-day living.

The World Land Trust (WLT) works to save tropical forests and undertakes reforestation in areas that have been cleared. But the fact remains that an area equivalent to 50 football fields of tropical forest is being lost every minute, so there is no time to waste.

WHAT YOU CAN DO...

● Buy an acre of rainforest through the WLT, which will be protected in perpetuity by local partner organisations. Already WLT has helped save over 300,000 acres of tropical forests and other threatened habitats which would have been lost forever. www.worldlandtrust.org.

● Visit WLT's Carbon Balanced website to see how you can reduce your impact on the environment and help save endangered species by providing secure forest habitats.

WORLD LAND TRUST™

RED-BREASTED GOOSE

'THE EFFECTS OF GLOBAL WARMING ON THEIR BREEDING GROUNDS MAY RESULT IN THE EXTINCTION OF THE RED-BREASTED GOOSE' WWT

Probably the most striking of all geese, the red-breasted goose is easily recognisable by its distinctive red, black and white plumage. In 1996 the global population was estimated at 88,000 birds. Numbers may now have dwindled to 40,000, probably due to extremes of weather on the wintering grounds, and poor breeding conditions.

The main threats to the species are land-use changes, illegal hunting, and disturbance from hunting. The World Conservation Monitoring Centre has suggested that the effects of global warming on the breeding grounds may also result in the extinction of the red-breasted goose.

The Wildfowl & Wetlands Trust (WWT) is committed to an integrated conservation programme for the goose. This includes monitoring winter numbers, introducing hunting patrols; identifying and protecting preferred inland feeding sites; the formulation of a crop-rotation plan and a satellite-tracking project.

WHAT YOU CAN DO...

- Help fund the conservation of the red-breasted goose by becoming a member of WWT. Join online at www.wwt.org.uk/membership, call +44 (0) 1453 891195 or email: membership@wwt.org.uk.
- WWT is the only UK charity solely dedicated to saving wetlands and their wildlife on an international basis. Find out more about the charity and its nine UK visitor centres on +44 (0) 1453 891900, or at www.wwt.org.uk.

FACT BOX

COMMON NAME: Red-breasted goose

SCIENTIFIC NAME: *Branta ruficollis*

STATUS: Vulnerable

POPULATION: In 1996 the global population of red-breasted geese was at least 88,000 birds. This number fell to 40,000 birds by January 2004.

LIFESPAN: They probably live an average of 10-15 years in the wild, although in captivity up to 21 years.

RANGE: Up to 70% of red-breasted geese congregate at just two roost sites on the Shabla and Durankulak lakes on the Black Sea coast of north-east Bulgaria. Others areas are in Ukraine, Romania and southern Russia. Staging grounds in Kazakhstan. Breeding grounds in arctic Russia.

THREATS: Dependence on a very small number of winter roosts where land-use change (shift from winter wheat to crops unsuitable as food), illegal hunting, disturbance from hunting and climate change affect numbers.

 WWT Wildfowl & Wetlands Trust

RED RUFFED LEMUR

'UNLESS THE ISLAND IS STABILISED QUICKLY, EXTINCTION OF LEMURS IN THE WILD ON MADAGASCAR IS A REAL POSSIBILITY IN THE NEXT 50-60 YEARS' LEMUR CONSERVATION FOUNDATION

Red ruffed lemurs are among the most exquisite and charismatic of the endangered lemurs. Madagascar, home to all lemurs, is considered one of the most ecologically diverse and important regions on the planet. However, the island has lost about 90% of its forest since the arrival of man almost 2,000 years ago and is currently losing its forested habitat at the rate of about 1% per year due to human activities.

This critical loss of habitat and the hunting of lemurs for food and because they are seen as crop pests make the outlook for these primates fairly poor. Red ruffed lemurs are restricted to only one small region of Madagascar and suffer the same threats as other lemurs.

Current changes underway to stem this loss give some reason for hope, but unless the island is stabilised quickly, extinction of lemurs in the wild on Madagascar is a real possibility in the next 50-60 years.

WHAT YOU CAN DO...

● Discover what the Lemur Conservation Foundation is doing to help conserve red ruffed and other lemurs by visiting www.lemurreserve.org.

● Be mindful that all beings, including humans, are part of the complex web of life. While we can think of red ruffed lemurs in Madagascar and wish to protect them, we can be equally sensitive to the environmental needs in our own backyard – 'Think globally, act locally!'. Every person can make a difference in sustaining life on earth if we have the courage to face problems and the will to help solve them.

FACT BOX

COMMON NAME: Red ruffed lemur

SCIENTIFIC NAME: *Varecia rubra*

STATUS: Endangered

POPULATION: According to a 1997 survey, there were about 15,000 red ruffed lemurs of breeding age in the wild.

LIFESPAN: Fifteen to 20 years in the wild

RANGE: Red ruffed lemurs live in a very restricted area, mostly in the Masoala National Park (840sq.m) on the Masoala Peninsula in north-eastern Madagascar. Within that region, red ruffed lemurs have home ranges of about 58 hectares.

THREATS: Red ruffed lemurs are losing their habitat, they are hunted for food, and are subject to severe environmental distress, such as cyclones, which often hit this area of Madagascar

LEMUR CONSERVATION FOUNDATION

RINGED SEALS

'ALL THE SPECIES OF RINGED SEAL IN THE EASTERN EUROPEAN LAKES HAVE SUFFERED POPULATION DECLINES OF MORE THAN 75% IN A CENTURY' SEAL CONSERVATION SOCIETY

From the northern Baltic, stretching east across Finland and Russia, there is a series of landlocked water bodies: Lakes Ladoga, Saimaa, Baikal and the Caspian Sea and the northern Baltic sea.

The original numbers of these seals was roughly proportional to the size of the lake, the largest being the Caspian, with an estimated million seals around 1900, while the smallest was Saimaa, with a population in 1900 of only 1,000. All these seals have declined dramatically by more than 75% since 1900. The main cause of the decline has been hunting of whitecoat pups (and often adults). In addition, the accidental catching of pups in fishing gear is a particular threat to the Saimaa and Ladoga seals, while the Baltic and Caspian seals suffer low fertility due to organochlorine pollutants, and epidemics of the canine distemper virus. The population of Baltic, Saimaa and Ladoga seals has stabilised now due to conservation measures, but the Caspian seal is still declining.

WHAT YOU CAN DO...

● Check the Seal Conservation Society's website www.pinnipeds. org for ongoing news and ways of lending support.

● Visit, too, www.sealresearch.org. The website of the Finnish Association for Nature Conservation, www.sll.fi, provides information on the wildlife of Finland.

FACT BOX

COMMON NAMES: Baltic ringed seal; Ladoga seal; Saimaa seal; Caspian seal (pictured): Baikal seal

SCIENTIFIC NAMES: *Phoca (Pusa) hispida botnica; P. h. ladogensis; P. h. saimensis; P. caspica: P. sibirica*

STATUS: Vulnerable (Baltic): vulnerable (Ladoga): endangered (Saimaa): vulnerable (Caspian): due for review in 2006): lower risk/near threatened (Baikal)

POPULATION: 6,000 (Baltic): 5,000 (Ladoga): 270 (Saimaa): 111,000 (Caspian), a few tens of thousands (Baikal).

LIFESPAN: maximum longevity about 50 years in Baikal and Caspian and 40 years in Saimaa, Ladoga and Baltic.

RANGE: only in the isolated lakes and seas.

THREATS: Hunting, fisheries by-catch, organochlorine pollution (lowered fertility), disease epidemics; industrial development.

Seal Conservation Society

ROSEATE TERN

'ONE OF EUROPE'S MOST BEAUTIFUL BREEDING SEABIRDS, THE ROSEATE TERN IS UNFORTUNATELY ALSO ITS RAREST AND MOST THREATENED'

BIRDWATCH IRELAND

I n summer, Ireland holds approximately 85% of the north-west European breeding population of 1,000 pairs of roseate tern, with over 700 pairs alone on Rockabill Island off Dublin. The remainder nest in Britain and north-west France, the only other European colonies being in the Azores.

The biggest threat facing the Irish population is the trapping of young birds at their wintering grounds along the coast of west Africa. In addition, roseate terns are hugely dependant on dwindling stocks of small fish, and are very sensitive to pollution and disturbance. There is also a shortage of suitable nesting sites, with habitat loss during the twentieth century leading to the species' inclusion on the Irish Red List.

To ensure their future, new colonies must be established outside current breeding strongholds, and trapping on the wintering grounds must cease.

WHAT YOU CAN DO...

● Dublin Bay, on the east coast of Ireland, is one of the best places in the world to see roseate terns. If you know of a colony near you, please encourage your government to protect it.

● To find out more about roseate terns or to join BirdWatch Ireland and support its conservation work, visit www.birdwatchireland.ie, call +353 (1) 281 9878 or write to BirdWatch Ireland, PO Box 12, Greystones, Co. Wicklow, Ireland.

FACT BOX

COMMON NAME: Roseate tern

SCIENTIFIC NAME: *Sterna dougallii*

STATUS: Red-listed in Ireland, EU Annex 1

POPULATION: Around 120,000-130,000 pairs worldwide; Europe holds 2,000 pairs, confined to Ireland, Britain, France and the Azores.

LIFESPAN: The oldest recorded individual was 21 years old.

RANGE: The threatened *dougallii* subspecies breeds only in the Atlantic, at colonies in Europe, North America, the Caribbean and South Africa. Other races breed in Australia, Japan, and at various sites in the Indo-Pacific region.

THREATS: Trapping on wintering grounds, lack of suitable nesting sites, reduction in fish stocks, human disturbance and marine pollution.

SAINT LUCIA PARROT

'THIS SPECIES IS A BEACON OF HOPE, SHOWING THAT BY CHANGING PEOPLE'S ATTITUDES AND HABITS, WILDLIFE CAN BE PRESERVED FOR THIS AND FUTURE GENERATIONS' RARE

Though still vulnerable, the endemic Saint Lucia parrot is a conservation success story.

In the 1970s, the species flickered on the brink of extinction. Threatened by habitat destruction, the illegal wild bird trade, and hunting, it was one of the rarest birds in the world, with perhaps as few as 150 parrots remaining. But through the dedicated efforts of the Saint Lucia Forestry Department and conservation groups, the species has rebounded and now numbers about 600.

By raising conservation awareness among the islanders, protected areas were established and laws enacted to protect the parrot and its rainforest habitat. It is now a symbol not just of island pride – the Saint Lucia parrot is the national bird – but something more. It is a beacon of hope showing that by changing people's attitudes and habits, endangered wildlife can be preserved for this and future generations.

FACT BOX

COMMON NAME: Saint Lucia parrot

SCIENTIFIC NAME: *Amazona versicolor*

STATUS: Vulnerable

POPULATION: Estimated at 600 (Saint Lucia Forestry Department)

LIFESPAN: Unknown in wild

RANGE: Endemic to the eastern Caribbean island of Saint Lucia with an estimated range of 140sq.km.

THREATS: Habitat destruction, illegal wild bird trade, hurricanes, formerly hunting.

WHAT YOU CAN DO...

● Visit Saint Lucia and join the Forestry Department's rainforest walk for an opportunity to see the Saint Lucia parrot and other species while contributing to the island's economy and conservation. (+1 758 450 2078)

● Find out more about the conservation of the Saint Lucia parrot and other species by going to Rare's website at www.rareconservation.org.

RARE
inspiring conservation

SCIMITAR-HORNED ORYX

'THESE IMPRESSIVE ANTELOPE ARE PERFECTLY ADAPTED TO ARID HABITAT; NOT, HOWEVER, TO PROLONGED DROUGHTS AND COMPETITION WITH DOMESTIC LIVESTOCK' **MARWELL PRESERVATION TRUST**

Scimitar-horned oryx were one of the last species of large mammal to become extinct in the wild in the late twentieth century. These impressive antelope are perfectly adapted to the arid habitat surrounding the great Sahara desert; however these adaptations did not protect them from the prolonged droughts, excessive hunting and competition with livestock, which resulted in their eradication from northern Africa.

Luckily, by the time the last remaining population disappeared, conservation initiatives were underway with large numbers maintained in captivity. In 1985, a project began to reintroduce the oryx to Bou Hedma National Park in Tunisia, and today oryx have been released to fenced protected areas in two other parks in Tunisia and to three locations in Morocco and Senegal. These initiatives are continuing with further releases planned for the future. The final aim is to see the oryx roaming free once again over the aridlands surrounding the Sahara.

FACT BOX

COMMON NAME: Scimitar-horned oryx

SCIENTIFIC NAME: *Oryx dammah*

STATUS: Extinct in the wild

POPULATION: Scimitar-horned oryx are extinct in the wild, but reintroductions to fenced protected areas have resulted in approximately 450 individuals in National Parks in north Africa. There are in the region of 2,000-3,000 scimitar-horned oryx in zoological institutions around the world.

LIFESPAN: Unknown in the wild, but they can live up to 28 years in captivity.

RANGE: Formerly north and south of Sahara in sub-desert habitat from the Atlantic coast to the Nile. Reintroduced populations exist in Tunisia, Morocco and Senegal.

THREATS: Over-hunting, habitat destruction, competition with domestic livestock, drought and political instability.

WHAT YOU CAN DO...

• Support the work of Marwell Preservation Trust (www.marwell.org.uk) by making a donation towards the scimitar-horned oryx conservation programme. The money raised will help Marwell to return the oryx to north Africa, protect its habitat and other species which live there.

• Find out more about wildlife in the Sahara Desert and the threats that it faces by logging on to www.saharaconservation.org.

MARWELL
PRESERVATION TRUST

SCOTTISH WILDCAT

'TODAY IT HAS BEEN ESTIMATED THAT PERHAPS ONLY 400 ANIMALS SURVIVE, LEAVING THE SCOTTISH WILDCAT CRITICALLY ENDANGERED' THE MAMMAL SOCIETY

It is unthinkable that the Scottish Highlands could be without their ultimate symbol of wilderness, the Scottish wildcat. And yet this may become a reality in only a few years, unless we take action now. After centuries of destruction of its habitat, hunting for its fur and persecution as vermin, which almost led to its extinction in the early-twentieth century, the Scottish wildcat is under quite a different, but equally grave, threat of extinction today.

After persecution lessened following World War I, allowing recolonisation of the Highlands, wildcats hybridised with domestic cats, resulting in a wide spectrum of hybrid forms, but few wildcats. Today, it has been estimated that perhaps

only 400 animals survive, leaving the Scottish wildcat critically endangered. Radical conservation action such as captive breeding may be the only way we can ensure the Scottish wildcat will survive in the current century and beyond.

WHAT YOU CAN DO...

● Support charities and organisations who are working for the conservation of the Scottish wildcat such as The Mammal Society (www.mammal.org.uk) and the Highland Wildlife Park (www.highlandwildlifepark.org).

● If you live within the wildcat's range, neuter your domestic cat and vaccinate it annually against common viral diseases.

FACT BOX

COMMON NAME: Scottish wildcat

SCIENTIFIC NAME: *Felis silvestris*

STATUS: Critically endangered

POPULATION: The global population of the wildcat is unknown, but the Scottish wildcat may number as few as 400 individuals.

LIFESPAN: Wildcats usually only survive for two to three years; few live beyond five years, but one has been studied for 10 years in the wild.

RANGE: The Scottish wildcat is confined to northern Scotland, but wildcats range through Europe, Africa, south-west and central Asia.

THREATS: Hybridisation with domestic cats, habitat loss and fragmentation, vulnerability to domestic cat diseases and exposure to pesticides.

THE **Mammal** SOCIETY

SEYCHELLES SHEATH-TAILED BAT

'ROOST SITES AND FORAGING AREAS MUST BE URGENTLY PROTECTED OTHERWISE THIS SPECIES WILL BECOME EXTINCT' NATURE SEYCHELLES

The Seychelles sheath-tailed bat is possibly the rarest bat in the world with just 30-100 individuals left. It is one of two mammals endemic to the granitic Seychelles, and its biology is mostly unknown. Once common, it underwent a precipitous decline during the twentieth century and is listed as critical.

Recent studies by Nature Seychelles, British universities and the Ministry of Environment indicate that previously known populations on Praslin and La Digue islands are most likely extinct, but two previously unknown roosts were recently discovered on the island of Mahe, which along with Silhouette island, is now the extent of the bat's range. The studies showed that the species prefers mature tree stands in coastal areas for foraging and that habitat destruction, roost disturbance and pesticides are probably the major contributors to its decline.

Roost sites and foraging areas must be urgently protected otherwise, quite simply, this species will become extinct.

FACT BOX

COMMON NAME: Seychelles sheath-tailed bat

SCIENTIFIC NAME: *Coleura seychellensis*

STATUS: Critical

POPULATION: Between 30-100 individuals

LIFESPAN: Unknown. So rarely is this bat seen, that these photos are virtually the only ones in existence.

RANGE: Mahe Island and Silhouette Island in the Seychelles.

THREATS: Habitat destruction, roost disturbance and pesticides.

WHAT YOU CAN DO...

• Become a member of Nature Seychelles, or volunteer your time if you are a conservation professional. Contact Nature Seychelles at Roche Caiman, PO Box 1310, Mahe, Seychelles. Tel: +248 601100. Fax: +248 601102. Email: nature@seychelles.net.

• Support the Seychelles sheath-tailed bat project or other conservation activities in Seychelles by providing project funding or by putting the organisation in touch with donors. Find out more at www.natureseychelles.org.

Nature SEYCHELLES

SHARP-TAILED SNAKE

'RESIDENTIAL DEVELOPMENT IS THE GREATEST THREAT TO THIS TINY AND HARMLESS SNAKE' ISLANDS TRUST FUND

The sharp-tailed snake likes to live on Canada's Vancouver Island and Gulf Island shorelines. Unfortunately, so does everyone else, and residential development is the greatest threat to this tiny, harmless snake.

We need to discover more about this reptile's habitat requirements, to better understand the size and extent of their populations. Once existing snake population sites are known, conservationists can develop community awareness and help landowners make wise land-use decisions.

Meanwhile, developers and property owners can protect the 30cm, pencil-thick snake by avoiding construction or use of vehicles, cars, pesticides, lawnmowers or weed-eaters in its habitat. Local people can keep pets under control, remove invasive plant species, restore native vegetation and consider creating natural habitat shelters for the snakes on their land. The presence of this species is indicative of over 100 threatened and endangered species in associated ecosystems.

FACT BOX

COMMON NAME: Sharp-tailed snake

SCIENTIFIC NAME: *Contia tenuis*

STATUS: Endangered in Canada (according to the Committee on the Status of Endangered Species in Canada)

POPULATION: Not known, but very rare in Canada.

LIFESPAN: Up to nine years in the wild.

RANGE: There are eight known populations from 17 sites, all within 50km of Victoria, BC (British Columbia).

THREATS: Habitat loss due to urban and residential development, habitat alteration by weeds, predation by introduced species, loss of tiny populations due to chance disturbances.

WHAT YOU CAN DO...

• Landowners can protect sunny, south-facing rocky slopes by leaving natural covers and hiding places, controlling invasive plants, avoiding pesticides and keeping cats indoors.

• The Islands Trust Fund (www.islandstrustfund.bc.ca) and the Habitat Acquisition Trust (www.hatbc.ca) welcome donations to assist them in protecting this rare habitat.

Islands Trust Fund

SIBERIAN CRANE

'CRANES ARE ONE OF THE MOST THREATENED FAMILIES OF BIRDS ON EARTH, THEIR POPULATIONS DECLINING FOR A NUMBER OF REASONS' INTERNATIONAL CRANE FOUNDATION

Worldwide, the sight and sound of cranes stir the spirit. Cranes are symbols of harmony, fidelity, longevity, good fortune and vigilance throughout many cultures on the five continents they inhabit. In spite of this, cranes are one of the most threatened families of birds on earth. Crane populations are declining for a variety of reasons, including illegal trade, human disturbance, political instability, pollution and environmental contamination, and power line collisions. The unmanaged loss and degradation of wetlands and grasslands is the single largest threat to these birds.

The Siberian crane is one of those most under threat. The species is now found in only two populations, the eastern and western. A central population of Siberian Cranes once nested in western Siberia and wintered in India. The last documented sighting of Siberian Cranes in India during the winter months was in 2002. Although there are credible reports of small numbers of birds in the western and central populations, all but a few existing birds belong to the eastern population.

WHAT YOU CAN DO...

• Become a crane 'parent' by adopting a crane through the International Crane Foundation (ICF) (www.savingcranes). Money raised helps ICF protect cranes and their ecosystems around the world.

• Learn about Siberian Crane Flyway Coordination established under UNEP/GEF Siberian Crane Wetlands Project and the Convention on the Conservation of Migratory Species Memorandum of Understanding Concerning Conservation Measures for the Siberian Crane at www.sibefly.org and www.scwp.info.

FACT BOX

COMMON NAME: Siberian crane

SCIENTIFIC NAME: *Grus leucogeranus*

STATUS: Critically endangered

POPULATION: Around 2,500-3,000 birds

LIFESPAN: The oldest documented crane that ever lived was a Siberian crane named Wolf, who died at the age of 83. Wolf is in the *Guinness Book of World Records*.

RANGE: The eastern population breeds in north-eastern Siberia and winters along the middle Yangtze river in China. The western population winters at a single site along the south coast of the Caspian Sea in Iran and breeds just south of the Ob river east of the Ural mountains in Russia.

THREATS: Loss and degradation of habitats along migratory routes (conversion of wetlands, dam and water diversions), development of resource industries in critical habitat, human disturbance, inadequate protected area management, pollution.

SNOW LEOPARD

'FEW SNOW LEOPARDS SURVIVE, SCATTERED ACROSS THE EXPANSE OF REMOTE AND RUGGED MOUNTAINS IN CENTRAL ASIA AND THE HIMALAYAS' CARE FOR THE WILD INTERNATIONAL

Mysterious and elusive, snow leopards are at home in one of the harshest and most inaccessible environments on earth, equipped with thick fur for protection against the climate, and a long, thick tail to act as counterbalance on sleep rocky terrain.

Withstanding freezing temperatures and icy winds at altitudes of up to 6,000m, these animals are defenceless against vicious steel traps and guns. Despite national and international laws to protect them, snow leopards have still been decimated by poaching for their pelts, skin and bones, which are traded illegally in at least 11 of the 12 countries in which they occur.

As herders graze their livestock higher into the mountains, the snow leopards' wild prey disappears. Shortage of prey forces some snow leopards to target livestock, leading to intensified persecution. In one of the worst areas, Care for the Wild International's elite anti-poaching unit has stopped the poachers in their tracks.

FACT BOX

COMMON NAME: Snow leopard

SCIENTIFIC NAME: *Uncia uncia*

STATUS: Endangered

POPULATION: Between 3,860-6,250 snow leopards are believed to survive, although most of the estimates that contributed to this total are many years out of date. Either way, snow leopards are even rarer than tigers.

LIFESPAN: Unknown in the wild, 21 years in captivity.

RANGE: Snow leopards have an extensive but fragmented range within the mountains of Afghanistan, Bhutan, China, India, Kazakhstan, Kyrgyzstan, Mongolia, Nepal, Pakistan, Russia, Tajikstan and Uzbekistan.

THREATS: Illegal hunting and trade in live animals, trophies and body parts, retaliation killings by farmers to protect livestock, human encroachment and disappearing natural prey.

WHAT YOU CAN DO...

● Adopt the two rescued snow leopards Alcu and Bagira (www.careforthewild.com or +44 (0) 1306 627900). Your money will help CWI provide care for rescued or injured snow leopards as well as protect the species in the wild.

● Find out more about CWI's wildlife protection work around the world by visiting www.careforthewild.com, or by phoning +44 (0) 1306 627900.

SONORAN PRONGHORN

'THIS SUBSPECIES TEETERS AT THE EDGE OF EXTINCTION WITH ONLY APPROXIMATELY 500 ANIMALS KNOWN TO REMAIN IN THE WILD?'

SIERRA CLUB

The herds of pronghorn dancing across the North American grasslands are one of the natural world's greatest works of art. Distinguished by its branched horns, the pronghorn population fell from about 40-50 million animals ranging from Canada to Mexico at the time of European colonisation to a mere 12,000 at the beginning of the twentieth century, the result of commercial hunting and habitat loss. Today, thanks to the work of sport hunters who campaigned to end commercial hunting, there are now an estimated 1.1 million pronghorn (shown right) in the US. Yet the Sonoran pronghorn (below), a subspecies that inhabits the desert lands of the American Southwest and Mexico, still teeters at the edge of extinction with only about 500 known to remain in the wild. Fences which keep them away from important habitat, the loss of habitat to development, predation of fawns by coyotes and collisions with vehicles all jeopardise the existence of this remarkable part of America's heritage.

FACT BOX

COMMON NAME: Sonoran pronghorn

SCIENTIFIC NAME: *Antelocarpa americana*

STATUS: Endangered

POPULATION: There are an estimated 500 Sonoran pronghorn in the wild. Less than 30 are believed to range within the United States with the remainder thought to range in adjacent Mexico.

LIFESPAN: Nine years

RANGE: Pronghorns range exclusively in the grasslands of western North America, from Canada to Mexico. The Sonoran subspecies ranges in the deserts along the United States/Mexican border

THREATS: Fragmentation and destruction of habitat, predation of fawns by coyotes and collisions with automobiles.

SIERRA CLUB
FOUNDED 1892

WHAT YOU CAN DO...

● Find out more about the work of Sierra Club to conserve the Sonoran pronghorn by visiting www.sierraclub.org or by phoning +1 415 977 5500.

● The Sierra Club is involved in a wide range of conservation projects across many species. To find out more, visit www.sierraclub.org

SOUTH CHINA TIGER

'DRIVEN FROM ITS HOME AND HUNTED TO NEAR EXTINCTION, FEWER THAN 100 OF THESE MAGNIFICENT ANIMALS ARE LEFT ALIVE TODAY'

SAVE CHINA'S TIGERS

Save China's Tigers

The Chinese tiger is the most endangered of the five remaining subspecies of tiger and the smallest. In the 1950s, there were 4,000 tigers in China. Due to hunting and habitat destruction, there are now fewer than 100 left.

What a terrible fate for the subspecies generally acknowledged to be the ancestor of all modern tigers.

The Chinese tiger used to live all over central and south China, but due to human intervention over the past few thousand years, it has slowly retreated to remote and mountainous areas south of the Yangtze River. It is an adaptable animal and managed its prosperous existence until humans took over their last bit of land – the mountains.

The aim of Save China's Tigers is to raise awareness of the plight of the Chinese tiger and to strive for its protection and preservation through public education, introduction and advanced conservation models in China.

FACT BOX

COMMON NAME: South China tiger

SCIENTIFIC NAME: Panthera tigris amoyensis

STATUS: Critically endangered

POPULATION: Estimates put the wild Chinese tiger population at between 10-30, while approximately 60 survive in Chinese zoos.

LIFESPAN: On average, tigers will live for 10-15 years out in the wild, and 16-20 years in captivity.

RANGE: In the wild last known south of the Yangtze River, south China.

THREATS: Hunting and habitat destruction

WHAT YOU CAN DO...

● Join the organisation to help raise awareness by adopting a tiger, making a donation or joining the tiger club.

● For further information on Save China's Tigers, please visit the website www.savechinastigers.org or call +44 (0) 20 7451 1296.

SPINY SEAHORSE

'THE COLLECTION OF SEAHORSES FROM THE WILD NEEDS TO BE BANNED' THE SEAHORSE TRUST

Seahorses conjure up images of creatures of myth and legend, a creature that is found pulling the chariot of Neptune or on ancient coats of arms and manuscripts. So it comes as a major surprise to many people to find there is not just one but two species of seahorse in the European waters of Britain. The spiny seahorse is the larger of the two – about six inches long with an impressive mane.

Seahorses are under threat throughout all the ranges where they are found. They are collected for a variety of trades, and in addition, they are disappearing from parts of their ranges due to pollution, habitat loss and sedimentation, which smothers the habitat they dwell in, killing off everything that lives there.

Traditionally, they have been associated with seagrass beds, but research by The Seahorse Trust through The British Seahorse Survey shows they can occupy quite a wide range of algae-covered areas and these areas need to be protected.

WHAT YOU CAN DO...

● Don't buy dried seahorses or starfish, shells or other marine creatures offered for sale by seaside shops. Also, don't buy wild caught seahorses as pets as they will not survive without specialist care.

● Find out more about The Seahorse Trust and the work it does through the British Seahorse Survey. Visit www.theseahorsetrust.co.uk and www.britishseahorsesurvey.org, email: neil.seahorses@tesco.net, or call +44 (0) 1392 875930.

FACT BOX

COMMON NAME: Spiny seahorse

SCIENTIFIC NAME: *Hippocampus guttulatus*

STATUS: Endangered and data deficient

POPULATION: Not entirely known, but not considered to be common.

LIFESPAN: In captivity, up to seven years and three months, but usually only a couple of years. In the wild, the lifespan is probably between six and seven years.

RANGE: All around Ireland, along the south coast of England, up the west coast around Wales as high as the Shetland Isles above Scotland. In Europe, found off the coasts of France, Belgium, Holland, Spain, Portugal and the Bay of Biscay and throughout the Mediterranean and the Black Sea.

THREATS: Seahorses worldwide are under major threat from over-fishing for the traditional medicine, pet and curio trades. They are also under major threat through habitat loss, pollution and as a bycatch in the fishing industry.

The Seahorse Trust

SUMATRAN RHINO

'THE SUMATRAN RHINO IS THE WORLD'S RAREST LARGE MAMMAL AND THE CLOSEST RELATIVE OF THE WOOLLY RHINOCEROS OF THE ICE AGE' SAVE THE RHINO INTERNATIONAL

In former times, Sumatran rhinos roamed freely from the foothills of the Himalayas in Bhutan and India through Myanmar, Thailand, Malaysia, Sumatra and Borneo. They are well-adapted to life in dense tropical forest, both lowland and highland, and used to be so numerous that they were regarded as garden pests. However, over the centuries, the Sumatran rhino has been exterminated over most of its range. Today only about 300 survive.

Since about 1995, poaching has become less of a problem, thanks to the establishment of Rhino Protection Units in major rhino areas. Habitat destruction in the name of agriculture and development is now the major threat to the Sumatran rhino. With strict protection, however, of both the remaining rhinos and their habitat, over the next century the populations could recover to at least 2,000 to 2,500 individuals; the number determined by population biologists as a minimum requirement for long-term survival of the species.

FACT BOX

COMMON NAME: Sumatran rhino, hairy rhino

SCIENTIFIC NAME: *Dicerorhinus sumatrensis* (From the Greek *di*, meaning two, *cero*, meaning horn and *rhinos*, meaning nose; *sumatrensis*, from Sumatra.)

STATUS: Critically endangered

POPULATION: About 300

RANGE: Sumatra, peninsular Malaysia and Sabah (northern Borneo). Scattered remnants are reported in remote and inaccessible parts of Thailand and Myanmar.

LIFESPAN: Sumatran rhinos are estimated to live an average of 30-45 years in the wild; while the longevity record for those in captivity is almost 33 years.

THREATS: Poaching for the horn (for use in traditional Chinese medicine) and habitat loss.

WHAT YOU CAN DO...

● Become a member of Save the Rhino International and help raise money to continue to support the work of the Rhino Protection Units. Visit the website, www.savetherhino.org, or telephone +44 (0) 20 7357 7474.

● Make sure that any hardwood furniture or floors you buy is certified by the Forestry Stewardship Council (FSC), and lobby your supermarket to source palm oil products from sustainable plantations.

TADPOLE SHRIMP

'THE CONSERVATION OF THIS SPECIES IS IMPORTANT, AS IT IS ONE OF THE OLDEST KNOWN SPECIES ON EARTH TODAY'
FRESHWATER BIOLOGICAL ASSOCIATION

The tadpole shrimp is known as a 'living fossil', because it doesn't appear to have changed since it first appeared in the fossil record over 200 million years ago. It lives in temporary pools, so the eggs are adapted to deal with this harsh environment. They can avoid desiccation, remaining dormant for up to several decades and hatch when pools refill with water. It is thought that *Triops* is disadvantaged in permanent water bodies and only thrives where other species cannot. Because of the unpredictable environment in which they live, tadpole shrimps have an incredibly rapid life cycle, the young reaching maturity in two to three weeks.

It is hard to know how endangered this species is, as populations may remain undiscovered until dry ponds or pools fill with water and individuals hatch. However, the conservation of this species is important, as it is one of the oldest known species on Earth today.

WHAT YOU CAN DO...

● Become a member of the Freshwater Biological Association (FBA), an international charity committed to promoting freshwater biology through scientific meetings, publications and research. For more information on how to join go to www.fba.org.uk or call +44 (0) 1539 442468.

● Visit www.freshwaterlife.org, an initiative of the FBA, to find out more information on all aspects of freshwater habitats and species.

FACT BOX

COMMON NAME: Tadpole shrimp

SCIENTIFIC NAME: *Triops cancriformis*

STATUS: Endangered (GB)

POPULATION: Exact numbers of *T. cancriformis* are not known, mainly because new populations will appear unexpectedly if dried-up ponds or pools refill with water. Eggs can survive for decades before being activated.

LIFESPAN: They usually live for between 20-70 days.

RANGE: This species can be found throughout Europe and into Russia in the east, and from the Middle East into India.

THREATS: These are thought to include water pollution, changes in management of pools, predation by ducks and fish, and the introduction of non-native plant species.

FRESHWATER BIOLOGICAL ASSOCIATION

Freshwater*Life*
Providing easy access to a world of freshwater information
www.freshwaterlife.org
info@freshwaterlife.org   +44 15394 42468

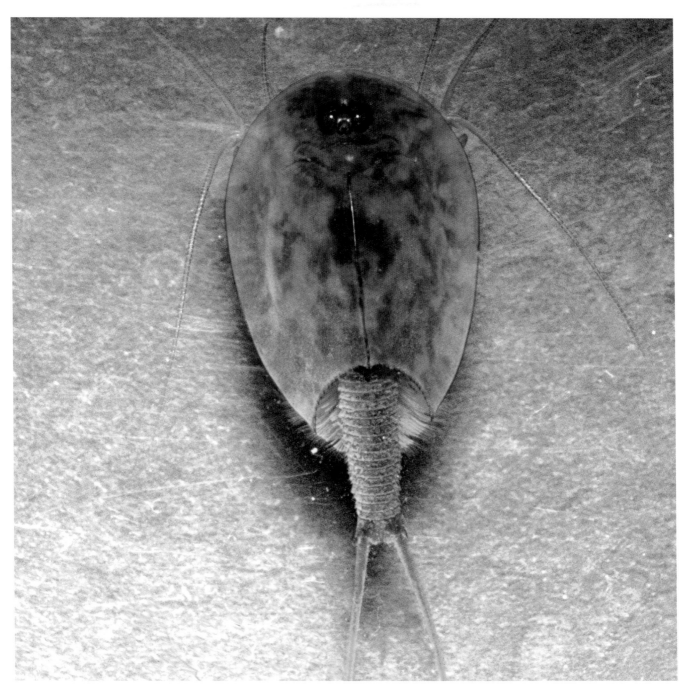

TASMANIAN WEDGE-TAILED EAGLE

'THIS EAGLE COULD BE ON THE BRINK OF EXTINCTION IN TASMANIA
IF LOGGING OF THE STATE'S OLD-GROWTH FORESTS CONTINUES'
THE WILDERNESS SOCIETY AUSTRALIA

Big enough to hunt kangaroos, Tasmania's wedge-tailed eagles are a rare subspecies of Australia's largest bird of prey. Monarchs of the forest, they can soar more than 2km above the ground, and identify prey from over 1.5km away. They live in nests atop some of the highest trees in Tasmania's old-growth forests – the tallest hardwood forests on Earth.

But perhaps not for much longer. Farmers shoot them, and logging companies clearcut their forests and export the wood to Japan's paper-making factories.

It is estimated that there are now fewer than 1,500 Tasmanian wedge-tailed eagles left, including fewer than 500 breeding pairs. They are listed by the Australian government as endangered.

Breeding pairs, who mate for life, usually produce only one egg per year, and only half of these survive.

FACT BOX

COMMON NAME: Tasmanian wedge-tailed eagle

SCIENTIFIC NAME: *Aquila audax fleayi*

STATUS: Endangered

POPULATION: Fewer than 1,500 birds; fewer than 500 breeding pairs

LIFESPAN: Over 20 years

RANGE: Australian state of Tasmania

THREATS: Logging, shooting and land-clearing. To make matters worse, loggers poison native marsupials such as wallabies to stop them feeding on regrowing saplings, and the poison is passed on to the eagles which feed on their carcasses. The long-term impacts of this diet on the eagles' physiology and longevity are not known.

WHAT YOU CAN DO...

● Visit The Wilderness Society Australia's website to find out more about the campaign to protect Tasmania's old-growth forests and wildlife: www.wilderness.org.au.

● Please write to the Australian Prime Minister, Parliament House, Canberra ACT 2600, Australia, asking him to protect Tasmania's old-growth forests.

THE WILDERNESS SOCIETY

TELMATOBIUS GIGAS

'T. GIGAS HAS ITS LAST REMAINING POPULATIONS CONFINED WHOLLY TO A SINGLE UNPROTECTED AREA, MAKING IT A PRIORITY FOR IMMEDIATE CONSERVATION ACTION' CONSERVATION INTERNATIONAL

Species of the genus *Telmatobius* constitute a remarkable group of frogs endemic to the Andes region of South America. Unfortunately, it is also a group of species at severe risk of immediate extinction. *Telmatobius gigas* lives in streams in high-elevation puna grassland habitats, where it presumably breeds by larval development in flowing water. Although undoubtedly affected by ongoing habitat loss and the effects of water pollution, *T. gigas* has also been subject to overharvesting for medicinal use.

Furthermore, the biology and ecology of this species make it particularly susceptible to infection by the pathogenic fungus that causes chytridiomycosis, which has devastated amphibian populations in Central and South America. *T. gigas* is one of many highly threatened species with their last remaining populations confined wholly to a single unprotected area, making species such as this priorities for immediate conservation action.

FACT BOX

COMMON NAME: No common name

SCIENTIFIC NAME: *Telmatobius gigas*

STATUS: Critically endangered

POPULATION: Although the worldwide population is unknown, and *T. gigas* is confined to a single locality, it is apparently common at this locality.

LIFESPAN: Unknown

RANGE: This species is known to only inhabit canyons of the Río Huayllamarca, in Carangas Province, Oruro Department, in the Bolivian Andes, at around 3,965m above sea level.

THREATS: Habitat loss; water pollution from agriculture; overharvesting for medicinal use; and stream canalisations for crop irrigation. Disease (chytridiomycosis) is a potential future threat.

WHAT YOU CAN DO...

● Find out more about Conservation International and *Telmatobius gigas* at www.conservation.org.

● Discover more about other threatened amphibians at www.globalamphibians.org and www.iucnredlist.org.

CONSERVATION INTERNATIONAL

TRINIDAD PIPING-GUAN

'HUNTING AND HABITAT LOSS HAS DRIVEN GUAN NUMBERS DOWN: THEY ARE NOW AT RISK OF EXTINCTION' WORLD PHEASANT ASSOCIATION

Did you know that cracids are threatened? Do you even know what a cracid is? Should you be worried about them?

Cracids are a group of about 50 medium to large-bodied bird species from the Neotropics, where they are often heavily hunted and therefore at risk of extinction in many places. The Trinidad piping-guan is one of the most threatened species, although a misleading picture is given by habituated birds often seen by visiting birdwatchers. A combination of hunting and habitat loss has driven numbers down so that it is difficult to encounter outside the one or two places where the species is regularly seen by birdwatching groups.

Recent conservation initiatives have seen the species designated as an Environmentally Sensitive Species and part of its geographic range an Environmentally Sensitive Area. Despite these advances, and the gathering of new information, it remains poorly known and in perilously low numbers.

WHAT YOU CAN DO...

● Promote responsible birdwatching tourism in Trinidad so that local communities benefit from the interest and money that the pawi (as it is known locally) brings.

● Join the World Pheasant Association and support its work on critically endangered species by visiting www.pheasant.org.uk or by phoning +44 (0) 1425 657 129.

FACT BOX

COMMON NAME: Trinidad piping-guan, or pawi (local name)

SCIENTIFIC NAME: *Pipile pipile*

STATUS: Critically endangered

POPULATION: Very difficult to determine reliably, but the species' range is only about 150km^2 in suitable habitat, where it is thought that there are fewer than 200 individuals remaining.

LIFESPAN: Not known

RANGE: Known only from the Northern Range in north-eastern Trinidad, West Indies.

THREATS: Habitat loss and hunting across its limited range.

TSODILO DAISY

'THE TSODILO DAISY IS EXTREMELY RARE, DOWN TO JUST A FEW INDIVIDUALS' THE ROYAL BOTANIC GARDENS, KEW

The Tsodilo daisy is very similar in appearance to its close relative *Erlangea misera* and also to several of the locally common *Vernonia* species. However, it is extremely rare, down to just a few individuals. It is one of only about 20 species that are endemic to Botswana and is therefore of national importance. The Tsodilo hills, where it occurs, are an important tourist destination, as well as being sacred to the San people (Bushmen). There are three hills described in Bushman folklore as the male hill, the female hill and the child. *Erlangea remifolia* grows on just one of these hills and is currently tucked away out of sight of the tourists who come to see Tsodilo's rock art.

Kew's Millennium Seed Bank Project has been working with partner institutions in Botswana to collect and bank the seed of rare and threatened plants in Botswana since 2003. Seed from the Tsodilo daisy was collected in the project's first year, and is now safely banked in both Botswana and the UK.

WHAT YOU CAN DO...

• Support the Millennium Seed Bank Project, which aims to collect and conserve seed of 10% of the world's wild plant species by 2010. Tel. +44 (0) 1444 894035.

• Find out more about the work of the Millennium Seed Bank Project at www.kew.org/msbp.

FACT BOX

COMMON NAME: Tsodilo daisy

SCIENTIFIC NAME: *Erlangea remifolia*

SIZE: 20-100cm tall

POPULATION: Just a few remaining individuals.

LIFESPAN: The Tsodilo daisy is a perennial or long-lived annual.

RANGE: Restricted to the Tsodilo hills area of north-western Botswana. This species can only be found on one of the three main hills in the district.

THREATS: Tourism and development. The Millennium Seed Bank team in Botswana, together with the authorities who manage Tsodilo, continue to monitor the status of this population.

Kew

PLANTS PEOPLE POSSIBILITIES

WATER VOLE

'THE WATER VOLE IS BRITAIN'S FASTEST DECLINING MAMMAL BUT ITS PLIGHT HAS GONE UNNOTICED FOR THE MAJORITY OF THE LAST CENTURY' THE WILDLIFE TRUSTS

Many people in the UK will have read *The Wind in the Willows* by Kenneth Grahame, and no doubt adored 'Ratty' the water vole, one of the heroes of the story. However, the water vole has declined by around 89% over the last century (a faster pace than the rhinos in Africa) and the loss has largely gone unnoticed. Loss of wetlands through drainage, increased agricultural production and canalisation of watercourses (placement of hard materials along the edges of rivers and streams) has severely reduced the amount of habitat where water voles can live.

American mink, a non-native predator brought to Britain for the fur trade during the 1930s, and now established in the countryside, threatens to consume surviving water vole colonies. Although conservation work is underway to help protect the remaining populations, there is still much more that can be done to help the water vole and bring it back from the edge of extinction.

FACT BOX

COMMON NAME: Water vole

SCIENTIFIC NAME: *Arvicola terrestris*

STATUS: UK Biodiversity Action Plan Priority Species, severely declined

POPULATION: Exact British population is unknown, there are still some large colonies surviving and there is ongoing monitoring work by several conservation organisations in the UK.

LIFESPAN: Average lifespan in the wild is nine months, but they are known to live for up to three years.

RANGE: *Arvicola terrestris* is found only in England, Scotland and Wales. A similar subspecies is found in continental Europe.

THREATS: Habitat loss and predation by American mink.

WHAT YOU CAN DO...

● **Help to survey water voles.** The Wildlife Trusts (www.wildlifetrusts.org) is one of many organisations which help to monitor water vole populations around Britain. This will help to establish whether or not surviving populations are still threatened by habitat loss and American mink.

● **Join your local Wildlife Trust.** The Wildlife Trusts is a partnership of 47 local Wildlife Trusts across the UK, plus the Isle of Man and Alderney. For further information, visit www.wildlifetrusts.org.

WHALE SHARK

'WHALE SHARKS ARE THE GENTLE GIANTS OF THE TROPICAL OCEANS'
MARINE CONSERVATION SOCIETY, SEYCHELLES

Whale sharks are the largest living fish in the world's oceans, and like their namesakes the whales, they feed on zoo-plankton, some of the smallest animals in the sea. For those who have been lucky enough to see these magnificent gentle creatures, there can be no doubt that they are one of the most charismatic of all the ocean's species.

Born at around 60cm, they are most frequently seen at sizes of four metres to eight metres, weighing from 500kg to 6,500 plus kg; the largest reliably recorded was 20m long and weighed 34,000 kg. But for all their size the species is now in peril as unrestricted fishing of these sharks to provide 'Tofu' shark for Asian restaurants has brought regional populations to the brink of collapse around Taiwan, the Philippines and India. The species has now been listed on Appendix II of Cites, requiring international trade to be recorded, but direct action to stop the hunting of whale sharks is needed if this long-lived species is to survive in the world's tropical oceans.

WHAT YOU CAN DO...

● Adopt a whale shark. Visit the Marine Conservation Society, Seychelles (www.mcss.sc). The money helps MCSS fund its whale shark monitoring activities and regional whale shark awareness programme.

● Find out more about whale sharks and the regional and international efforts to monitor and conserve the species by subscribing to its free online whale shark monitoring newsletter 'Sagren' on the MCSS website (www.mcss.sc).

FACT BOX

COMMON NAME: Whale shark

SCIENTIFIC NAME: *Rhincodon typus*

STATUS: Vulnerable

POPULATION: The worldwide population of whale sharks is unknown; data from Western Australia indicates a population of around 670-1,300 in that area, and from Seychelles of around 488 to 1,015 whale sharks.

LIFESPAN: It is currently thought that whale sharks can live to around 147 years of age, and are not reproductively mature until they reach 21 years.

RANGE: Principally occurring in tropical and warm temperate seas from 30°N to 30°S, but they have also been recorded outside of these latitudes in areas off South Africa between 30-35°S, and off New Zealand between 34-38°S.

THREATS: Targeted fishing, collision with boats and also getting entangled in fishing nets.

WHITE-BACKED VULTURE

'ONCE THE MOST ABUNDANT LARGE BIRD OF PREY IN INDIA, THIS MAJESTIC SPECIES HAS RECENTLY UNDERGONE A CATASTROPHIC POPULATION DECLINE' RSPB

Oriental white-backed vultures in South Asia have suffered one of the most rapid and widespread population declines of any bird species in history, with numbers plummeting by over 97% in the last 15 years. Along with the closely related long-billed and slender-billed species, the white-back has fallen victim to veterinary usage of the drug diclofenac, used to treat sick domestic livestock. The vultures are poisoned when they feed on animal carcasses.

The situation is critical and captive breeding programmes now being established are essential to try to rebuild the species' populations. Scientists from the RSPB and elsewhere have shown that meloxicam would be a suitable replacement for diclofenac because it is not toxic to vultures yet it is as equally effective in treating cattle.

Diclofenac was finally banned in 2006, but for the white-backed vulture, recovery is now a life or death situation, and extinction still a real possibility.

WHAT YOU CAN DO...

● Support the RSPB (www.rspb.org.uk). The RSPB needs your support to help wild birds and the places they live both in the UK and through international campaigns. The charity has lobbied for a ban by the Indian government on the use of diclofenac and is currently working with Indian conservationists to set up captive breeding centres.

● Spread the word about the plight of the vulture – the greater the awareness, the greater the support.

FACT BOX

COMMON NAME: White-backed vulture (Also known as white-rumped vulture and Indian white-backed vulture.)

SCIENTIFIC NAME: *Gyps bengalensis*

STATUS: Critically endangered

POPULATION: There are no known population estimates for this species, but it is thought that numbers have dipped to the low thousands in comparison to former figures in the millions.

LIFESPAN: The white-back vulture has an estimated lifespan of 25-30 years.

RANGE: This species was widespread until the late 1990s, when it was elevated to a critically endangered status.

THREATS: The overwhelming threat to the white-backed vulture is poisoning through eating dead cattle previously treated with diclofenac.

RSPB

for birds
for people
for ever

WOLLEMI PINE

'THE DISCOVERY OF THE WOLLEMI PINE IS THE EQUIVALENT OF FINDING A SMALL DINOSAUR STILL ALIVE ON EARTH'
WOLLEMI PINE CONSERVATION CLUB

The Wollemi pine is one of the world's oldest and rarest plants; it dates back to the time of the dinosaurs.

A member of the 200 million-year-old Araucariaceae family, the Wollemi pine was previously thought extinct, with only fossil records remaining. There are less than 100 wild adult Wollemi pines which have been protected in a secret location while an ex situ propagation programme has been underway to make the species commercially available. The commercialisation strategy, identified by the 'Wollemi Pine Recovery Plan', is designed to minimise unwanted visits to the wild population by making cultivated pines widely available, thereby funding conservation of the in situ population through royalties from the sale of every Wollemi pine.

It is one way that everyone who wishes to care for a Wollemi pine can participate in the global conservation effort.

WHAT YOU CAN DO...

• Grow your own Wollemi pine and play a role in one of the most significant comebacks in natural history. For information on how to acquire a pine, visit www.wollemipine.com or call +61 754 864 833.

• Join the Wollemi Pine Conservation Club to receive regular email updates on the latest news on research and conservation efforts. Visit www.wollemipine.com.

FACT BOX

COMMON NAME: Wollemi pine

SCIENTIFIC NAME: *Wollemia nobilis*

AGE: The Wollemi pine belongs to the 200 million-year-old Araucariaceae family. Relatives of the same family include the Norfolk Island pine, Kauri pine and Monkey Puzzle pine.

POPULATION: The exact location of the wild population (fewer than 100 mature trees) is a secret. It is the only known population in the world, and was discovered in 1994 in a remote rainforest gorge 200km west of Sydney (Australia) in the World Heritage Listed Blue Mountains.

GROWTH HABIT: Fast growing in light (up to 20m), favours slightly acidic soils, and can survive temperatures from -12 up to 45°C.

CONSERVATION: Royalties from sales of the Wollemi pine supports conservation of the pines and other rare and endangered plant species.

the
WOLLEMI
PINE

WOOLLY MONKEY

'WOOLLY MONKEYS' FOREST HABITAT IS INCREASINGLY FRAGMENTED, AND THEIR SURVIVAL IS ALSO THREATENED BY HUNTING FOR BUSHMEAT' THE MONKEY SANCTUARY TRUST

The woolly monkey is one of the largest and most beautiful of the South American primates. It lives in the middle and upper Amazon basin, to the west of the rivers Negro and Tapajos, but there are four subspecies of woolly monkey recognised and spread over Central and South America. They are arboreal, spending most of their time high in the canopy of the trees up to 150ft up. The most striking adaptation of a woolly monkey is an incredibly useful prehensile tail, which acts as a powerful fifth limb.

Woolly monkeys need large areas of primary forest to move around in. Unfortunately, their forest habitat is increasingly fragmented, and their survival is additionally threatened by hunting for bushmeat. Their babies are still sold into the pet trade by unscrupulous hunters. It is not known how many woolly monkeys survive in the wild today, but hopefully with greater awareness and education, these beautiful monkeys and their natural habitat can be saved.

FACT BOX

COMMON NAME: Woolly monkey

SCIENTIFIC NAME: *Lagothrix lagothricha*

STATUS: From near threatened to vulnerable depending on the subspecies

POPULATION: The exact populations of woolly monkeys in the wild is unknown.

LIFESPAN: About 25 years in captivity.

RANGE: Woolly monkeys live in isolated areas in the Amazon basin in Central and South America.

THREATS: Woolly monkeys are certainly the most threatened wherever they occur, due to their being a frequent target of the bushmeat trade and the fact that the species is adapted to primary forest. Deforestation, logging, hunting, and the exotic pet trade are all threats.

WHAT YOU CAN DO...

● Adopt-a-monkey (visit the website www.adoptamonkey.org). The money raised will help us to rescue more monkeys in need in the UK and abroad.

● Only buy wood certified by the Forestry Standards Commission (FSC). That way, you can ensure you are not contributing to the destruction of rainforest.

The Monkey Sanctuary Trust

Registered Charity Number 1102532

YELLOW-EYED PENGUIN

'THE BIRDS' EXISTENCE, PARTICULARLY ON MAINLAND NEW ZEALAND, IS FRAGILE' YELLOW-EYED PENGUIN TRUST

Fast and sleek, proud and upright, yet also the Charlie Chaplin of the animal world, yellow-eyed penguins are a New Zealand icon. But they are a threatened species, and their iconic status brings with it the need to protect this vulnerable penguin, and to sensibly manage opportunities to enjoy its unique character.

The birds' existence, particularly on mainland New Zealand, is fragile: having evolved in the absence of land-based mammalian predators they are vulnerable to predation. Nevertheless, they are an adaptable species, and after the almost complete loss of their forested nesting grounds they have adjusted well to modified habitats.

Penguin numbers on New Zealand's South Island have substantially increased from a low of 190 pairs in 1990 to an estimated 430 pairs in 2005-2006. We can do little about their food supply or natural marine predators, but we can keep them safe in a protected environment ashore.

WHAT YOU CAN DO...

• Find out more about the yellow-eyed penguin Trust by visiting www.yellow-eyedpenguin.org.nz.

• Become a member of, or make a donation to, the Yellow-eyed Penguin Trust and help save this unique penguin. You can do this online via the website.

FACT BOX

COMMON NAME: Yellow-eyed penguin

LATIN NAME: *Megadyptes antipodes*

STATUS: Endangered

POPULATION: An estimated 432 pairs on mainland New Zealand (2005), 200 pairs on Stewart Island (estimated 2000), 1200 pairs Sub-Antarctic Islands (estimated 1992)

LIFESPAN: At least 22 years

RANGE: Found only along the eastern coastline of the South Island of New Zealand, and on Stewart Island and the Sub-Antarctic islands of Auckland and Campbell.

THREATS: Introduced mammalian predators to mainland New Zealand such as dogs, cats, ferrets, stoats and livestock disturbance. Natural predators are sea lions and large predatory fish.

YELLOWHAMMER

'THE LOSS OF THE YELLOWHAMMER IS A VERY VISIBLE SIGN OF DECLINING FARMLAND BIODIVERSITY' BTO

The yellowhammer is a standard-bearer for the farmland birds that have been lost by the million in the last 30 years.

There is no suggestion that every yellowhammer in Europe will disappear any time soon but, for a bird that was probably present in every lowland village in the time of our grandparents, its loss is a very visible sign of declining farmland biodiversity.

Other British farmland birds that are of high conservation concern are cirl bunting (only 700 pairs left in the UK), corn bunting (down 86% since 1967), grey partridge (down 86%), skylark (down 59%) and tree sparrow (down 97%). The yellowhammer, with a decline of 55%, is highlighted here as it is a species easily recognised by many people.

The male is a cheerful yellow-headed bird, with a rattling 'little bit of bread and no cheese' song, whilst the female is a little more subdued.

WHAT YOU CAN DO...

- The British Trust for Ornithology, along with the Scottish Ornithologists' Club and BirdWatch Ireland, are starting a major new project to map the latest distribution of British and Irish birds. To get involved in this or other BTO surveys visit www.bto.org.

- Support the work of the BTO by becoming a member. Phone +44 (0) 1842 750050 or email info@bto.org.

FACT BOX

COMMON NAME: Yellowhammer

SCIENTIFIC NAME: *Emberiza citrinella*

STATUS: Red-listed species of conservation concern in the UK and declining significantly in the rest of Europe.

POPULATION: About 800,000 pairs in the UK. 1,000,000 pairs have disappeared since 1967.

LIFESPAN: Most chicks will not survive long enough to breed in the next summer. A typical lifespan is three years but the oldest on record for the BTO ringing scheme is 11 years and nine months.

RANGE: Breeds across northern Europe and Asia from Ireland to eastern Russia.

THREATS: Alongside many other specialist farmland birds, the species is being marginalised by our desire for our food to be grown more cheaply.

CONSERVATION GROUPS

CONSERVATION GROUPS CONTINUED

PHOTO ACKNOWLEDGEMENTS

AFRICAN ELEPHANT: IFAW/Duncan Willetts AFRICAN WILD DOG: Yancey Walker ALPINE IBEX: Istituto Oikos AMUR LEOPARD: Rob Dolaard and M Korinek ANCIENT WOODLAND: WTPL/Ted Green ANDEAN CONDOR: WCS ASIAN ELEPHANT: Jeremy Holden/FFI and Juan Pablo Moreiras/FFI ATLANTIC COD: Yves Lanceau/NHPA/photoshot ATLAS MOTH: Shripad Kulkarani AZRAQ KILLIFISH: Koji Kawai/Royal Society for the Conservation of Nature BARBARY MACAQUE: Eric Shaw BECHSTEIN'S BAT: Hugh Clark BENGAL TIGER: Martin Harvey/Alamy, JupiterImages BLACK-BROWED ALBATROSS: Ruedi Abbuehl BLACK RHINO: Mark Carwardine and Lucky Mavrondonis BOWHEAD WHALE: Glenn Willimas/Ursus/SeaPics.com BROWN HYENA: Ingrid Wiesel BUMBLEBEES: Sam Ashfield and Denis G BUTTON CORAL: Douglas Fenner CERULEAN WARBLER: Jim Zipp/Ardea.com Robert Royse CHEETAH: CCF CHIMPANZEE: Limbe Wildlife Centre/Pro Wildlife COCO-DE-MER: Peter Wyse Jackson COMMON HIPPOPOTAMUS: Phil Crosby (phil@ philcrosbyphotography.com) COMMON SKATE: Paul Kay/osf.co.uk Terry Jackson CORNCOCKLE: Andrew Byfield CUVIER'S BEAKED WHALE: Todd Pusser/ SeaPics.com Graeme Cresswell DALL'S PORPOISE: Robert L. Pitman/SeaPics.com DELHI SANDS FLOWER-LOVING FLY: Guy Bruyea DRILL: Mark Bowler/NHPA/Photoshot Arend de Haas EASTERN LOWLAND GORILLA: Andrew Crawley ENGLISH ELM: The Tree Council ETHIOPIAN WOLF: Owen Newman and Claudio Sillero/ EWCP EURASIAN LYNX: Pro Natura/Urs Tester and Karl Weber EUROPEAN STAG BEETLE: Jason Chapman/IACR-Rothamsted and Lucas Jeker GIANT PANDA: Jean Paul Ferrero/Ardea, WWF-Canon/ Susan A Mainka WWF-Canon/Michel Gunther (p213) GOLDEN CONURE: Keith Ewart/World Parrot Trust and Alison Hales/World Parrot Trust GOULDIAN FINCH: Steve Murphy GRAND CAYMAN BLUE IGUANA: John Binns GREAT BARRIER REEF: NASA Goddard Space Flight Centre and Charles Savall GREAT CRESTED NEWT: Froglife GREEN TURTLE: Pete Atkinson/NHPA/Photoshot, W Coles GREVY'S ZEBRA: M. Watson/Ardea, Rob Thompson/Earthwatch GREY NURSE SHARK: Valerie Taylor/Ardea www.speciesspotlight.com GURNEY'S PITTA: Kenneth W Fink/Ardea HAWAIIAN COTTON TREE: J.K. Obata/Center for Plant Conservation Noa Lincoln/Amy B.H. Greenwell Ethnobotanical Garden HEMIPHLEBIA DAMSELFLY: John Trueman JAGUAR: Tom & Pat Leeson/ Ardea, Pete Oxford) JAVAN LEAF MONKEY: Ernie Janes/NHPA/Photoshot JOCOTOCO ANTPITTA:

Doug Wechsler/ VIREO KIPUNJI: Tim Davenport/WCS LEATHERBACK TURTLE: Peter Richardson/MCS and Matthew Witt LITTLE WHIRLPOOL RAMSHORN SNAIL: Paul Sterry/Nature Photographers Ltd 'LONESOME GEORGE': Heidi Snell LONG-EARED OWL: Chris Sperring and Derick Scott MANGROVE FINCH: Greg Lasley MARINE IGUANA: Alex Hearn and Mark Whitwell MARSH FRITILLARY: Jim Asher and Martin Warren MEDITERRANEAN MONK SEAL: CBD Habitat/Michel Cedenilla MILKY STORK: David Behrens, Lim Kim Chye MONARCH BUTTERFLY: Jeffrey S Pippen and USDA-Agricultural Research Service MULGARA: A N T Photo Library/NHPA/Photoshot (both) NATTERJACK TOAD: Paul Edgar NORTHERN RIGHT WHALE: WDCS ORANGUTAN: Kenneth W Fink/Ardea PHILIPPINE EAGLE OWL: WLR Oliver PIPING PLOVER: Gordon Prince and Ian Saddler POLAR BEAR: M Watson/ Ardea, Gilles Pucheu PONDS: Richard Snow/Pond Conservation and Dr Steve Head/Pond Conservation POWELLIPHANTA 'AUGUSTUS': Department of Consevation (New Zealand) PYGMY HOG: Roland Seitre RAINFOREST: Elizabeth Bomford/Ardea, WLT/PFB/Kevin Schafer RED-BREASTED GOOSE: WWT RED RUFFED LEMUR: Noel Rowe RINGED SEALS: Sue Wilson and Pavel Erokhin ROSEATE TERN: Billy Clarke and Terry Flanagan SAINT LUCIA PARROT: Paul Butler/Rare and James Morgan, Durrell Wildlife Conservation Trust SCIMITAR-HORNED ORYX: Tania Gilbert SCOTTISH WILDCAT: Sue Searle, www. acornecology.co.uk SEYCHELLES SHEATH-TAILED BAT: Dr Justin Gerlach, AUSE 2004 SHARP-TAILED SNAKE: Christian Engelstoft SIBERIAN CRANE: International Crane Foundation, Baraboo, Wisconsin SNOW LEOPARD: Thorsten Harder SONORAN PRONGHORN: B. Moose Peterson/Ardea SOUTH CHINA TIGER: Paul Hilton SPINY SEAHORSE: Steve Trewhella and Francis Apesteguy, both courtesy of The Seahorse Trust SUMATRAN RHINO: Nico van Strien TADPOLE SHRIMP: Dr Roger Key (English Nature) and FBA TASMANIAN WEDGE-TAILED EAGLE: Dave Watts TELMATOBIUS GIGAS: Ignacio de la Riva TRINIDAD PIPING-GUAN: Aidan Keane/World Pheasant Association and Margaret Cooper WATER VOLE: Andrew Dore and Andrew Caird WHALE SHARK: Johannes Schwabe and Simon Rogers WHITE-BACKED VULTURE: Guy Shorrock WOOLLY MONKEY: The Monkey Sanctuary Trust YELLOW-EYED PENGUIN: Denis Paterson YELLOWHAMMER: Jill Pakenham/BTO and Tommy Holden/BTO

With thanks, too, to James Morgan, Durrell Wildlife Conservation Trust, for the photo of Lee Durrell.

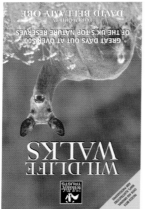